Advanced Stud
Expert S

Books in the series

Students' Guide to Business Computing
Students' Guide to Databases
Students' Guide to Data Communications
Students' Guide to Information Technology
Students' Guide to Office Automation
Students' Guide to Spreadsheets

Advanced Students' Guide to Expert Systems

Garry Marshall

Heinemann Newnes

Heinemann Newnes
An imprint of Heinemann Professional Publishing Ltd
Halley Court, Jordan Hall, Oxford OX2 8EJ

OXFORD   LONDON   MELBOURNE   AUCKLAND   SINGAPORE
IBADAN   NAIROBI   GABORONE   KINGSTON

First published 1990

© Garry Marshall 1990

British Library Cataloguing in Publication Data
Marshall, Garry, *1941–*
  Advanced students' guide to expert systems. – (Heinemann informatics series).
  1. Expert systems
  I. Title
  006.33

ISBN 0 434 91306 5

Typeset by BP Integraphics Ltd, Bath
Printed in Great Britain by Biddles of Guilford and Kings Lynn

Contents

Preface   vii

1: Introduction   1
Artificial intelligence: what it is and isn't – from AI to expert systems – what is an expert system and why is it needed? – areas of application and their characteristics – other related subjects

2: The principles of operation of expert systems   11
State transition model – expert system models – reviewing the situation – how to backtrack – a structure for expert systems

3: More on state spaces and search   33
The structure of state spaces – the implicit description of state spaces – search – some human factors

4: Making matters precise   48
Functions for handling lists – functions for searching – best-first search

5: Knowledge and ways of obtaining it   57
Eliciting knowledge from an expert – automatic means of elicitation – checking the knowledge obtained from examples – refining and analysing repertory grids

6: Knowledge representation and inference   82
Knowledge representation schemes – inference

7: Some expert systems   107
Classic systems – some other systems

Contents

8: Expert systems and tutoring — 128
Expert systems as browsers — tutorial systems

9: Dealing with uncertainty — 143
Knowledge representation and inference when there is no uncertainty — representation and inference with uncertainty

10: Languages for writing expert systems — 157
Prolog — Lisp

Annotated bibliography — 174
Index — 175

Preface

The Heinemann Informatics Series

This new series of books from Heinemann gives up-to-date coverage of significant developments in information technology. It is aimed at college students whose courses include IT components, including BTEC National and Higher Level courses, RSA and City & Guilds courses, as well as courses designed for professional bodies.

The books in this series adopt much more active learning strategies than traditional textbooks. Each chapter begins with a statement of what learning objectives the student is expected to achieve. At key points in a chapter the student is given the opportunity to achieve these objectives by carrying out short tasks, and by undertaking the assignment at the end of the chapter. Where appropriate, feedback on the tasks is provided at the end of a chapter, so that the student can assess his or her learning, and as a further check a résumé of the chapter's contents is given.

Most chapters include an assignment with a distinctly practical flavour. It may require the student to put his or her learning into practice using a computer or other item of IT equipment, or it may require an in-depth investigation into topics covered in the chapter.

Advanced Students' Guide to Expert Systems

Expert systems are studied in many subject areas, while seldom achieving real prominence in any of them. This may be because, until recently, the best-known users of expert systems were large computer companies and even larger oil companies. But the nature of expert systems is changing rapidly, to the point that they will soon be found alongside word processors, spreadsheets and databases in the personal computer market place. The resulting heightened profile will surely be reflected in an increase in the degree to which they are studied. The appearance of this book should prove timely.

Preface

The first three chapters of the book explain in broad terms what expert systems are and what they do, before going on to reveal the principles underlying their operation. Chapter 4 presents one approach to making the principles of operation precise. It includes some mathematics, but none that should frighten anyone. The chapter may, however, be skipped by the reader seeking no more than a general appreciation of expert systems. The basic ingredient of any expert system is knowledge: Chapter 5 looks at how it is obtained in the first place, and Chapter 6 considers how it can then be made available to the computer. Chapter 7 gives descriptions of operational expert systems, with the aim of showing how both knowledge and the principles of system operation have been treated in practice.

The next two chapters pursue avenues that follow from the existence of successful expert systems. These are, first, how the knowledge acquired for expert systems can be made available for teaching and training people and, second, how expert systems can cope in situations where knowledge is incomplete and some uncertainty exists. The final chapter (Chapter 10) is concerned with the essential step of describing a system design to a computer so that an expert system can be brought into existence. *Lisp* and *Prolog*, the main languages intended specifically for this purpose, are introduced. Chapters 4 and 9, respectively, have prepared the ground and, with this chapter, they should bring the reader who wishes to create an expert system to the point from which this task can be started.

My views on expert systems have been shaped in no small measure by members of staff of the Department of Computer Science at Brunel University. I owe them a debt of gratitude. I believe that their influence is evident in this book.

Computer software for use with this book

A number of expert system shells are available for the IBM PC and compatible computers. They include *Crystal* and *ExpertEase*. Any such program will be suitable for exploring the capabilities of an expert system. *TurboProlog*, *Golden Common Lisp* and *MuLisp* are also available for PCs, and are excellent vehicles for discovering *Prolog* and *Lisp*, as well as for writing expert systems. The reader with a Macintosh will find that *MacProlog* and *Procyon Common Lisp* are available for that computer. There are version of *TK!Solver* for the PC and for the Macintosh.

1: Introduction

Objectives

After reading this chapter, you should be able to:
- explain the concept of artificial intelligence
- describe how expert systems evolved from artificial intelligence
- define an expert system
- explain why expert systems can carry out tasks that conventional computer programs cannot
- outline the broad areas of application of expert systems
- appreciate the extent to which the foundations for expert systems draw on a number of established subjects.

Scenario

In a large office, the Chief Administrator of a busy National Health Service hospital is talking to the Head of Research.

'My doctors simply can't cope with all the patients we have to accept. I keep hearing about expert systems and that they can diagnose patients' illnesses. Do you know anything about them?'

'A little. We had one for evaluation recently.'

'Is there any chance we could introduce them to help reduce the work load on the doctors?'

Expert systems owe their origins to the area of study known as *artificial intelligence* (AI). As a subject, AI is not easy to define, but its main aim, very broadly, is to make computers do things that, if they were done by people, would be considered intelligent. Yet even this oversimplification raises a number of questions. What do we mean by intelligence? Why should we want computers to behave intelligently? What was wrong with the way computers did things already? It probably comes as no surprise to learn that AI is a subject of some controversy.

Over the years, as AI failed to deliver what it had promised, the original general and ambitious aims have been toned down. Its first products capable of practical application have been expert systems which, although they can be said to display intelligence, tend to operate in very restricted fields so that their intelligence is correspondingly restricted and far from general. In fact, it is something of a paradox that the computer can perform the same tasks as experts in their specialized domains well before it can even begin to carry out the sorts of things that most of us do without a second thought each and every day.

Expert systems are used to diagnose illnesses, to advise in the money markets, to configure computer systems, to help prospect for minerals and to supervise and even control military systems. We shall investigate the reasons that they are used in these applications both to see why conventional computing is not adequate and to discover why expert systems are appropriate. It will emerge that knowledge plays a key role, whether it is knowledge of how to recognise an illness or of how to recognize a threat from an enemy. Another important idea that will emerge is that it is appropriate to use expert systems in situations where some knowledge is available but complete knowledge is not.

Although the use of expert systems is a recent development, the study of knowledge is not. It has been a matter of interest to philosophers for a very long time, and the results of their thinking should be of more than passing interest to anyone involved with systems that manipulate knowledge. Artificial intelligence may be a newly minted subject, but it connects with areas that are very much older.

Artificial Intelligence: what it is and isn't

Artificial intelligence is the attempt to create computer programs that do intelligent things. The purposes of this activity are:

1 to investigate the nature of human intelligence
2 to model the processes underlying intelligence
3 to provide useful programs.

Attempts to reveal the nature of intelligence have met with little success,

Introduction

although they have proved stimulating. They aim to reveal the nature of human and computer intelligence just as aerodynamics explains how a bird flies and enables aeroplanes to be designed. The simulation of human intelligence is the site of much of the controversy about AI, essentially because it is difficult to distinguish between when a computer is *being* intelligent and when it is *simulating* intelligence. The point is that a computer can simulate intelligence without being intelligent in the same way as it can simulate the way in which water flows round an obstacle without being wet. The third aim has given rise to, amongst other things, expert systems.

If AI has had little success in revealing the nature of intelligence, it has led to an understanding of matters that we take for granted, including common sense, understanding what we see and appreciating readily the consequences of any change to our environment. AI has made contributions if only in revealing the complexity of these matters and in providing a basis for studying them further. Some progress has been made, although progress was not as great as it seemed at first. Newell and Simon's *General Problem Solver* did solve problems, but they turned out to be problems of a particular kind. Winograd's *SHRDLU* program maintained a world containing blocks of various colours and sizes. It could respond to enquiries about this world and obey commands to change it, both of which could be expressed in natural language. But the program has subsequently been criticized because its blocks world is so limited when compared to the richness of the real world that it can only be seen as a toy application operating in an environment so simple that it scarcely deserves to be called intelligent. One of the problems of AI is that real world situations are so complex: that is precisely why intelligence is needed. It has proved difficult to deal with these complexities and to keep track of the ramifications of even the smallest of changes to them. The situations that could be managed were, until recently at least, so simplified that it was hard to argue that they bore any relation to reality.

Another frustration for AI is that an aspect of intelligence can only be expressed as a computer program when it has been explained. Unexplained, intelligence appears mysterious but, as soon as it has been explained, it becomes mundane. This creates the catch that a program to display some facet of intelligence cannot be written until an explanation is available, but by then what it sets out to do is no longer impressive.

And why should we want computers to do the sort of things that people can do already? One answer is that the things people *want* to do are the things that people *do*. Some people, though, have knowledge, skills and

Advanced Students' Guide to Expert Systems

expertise that others do not. Is it not a good idea to make that skill and expertise readily available to anyone who might want access to it, or at least to make it more readily available than it otherwise would be? In any case, the expertise ought to be preserved in some form, for experts do not live for ever, and if their expertise is not preserved in some way it dies with them. Another way to answer the question is to observe that we do not want computers to do inhuman things. Also, if we want them to do the sort of things that people do not do, we might experience some difficulty in imagining what those things are!

As far as expert systems are concerned, though, the more esoteric aspects of all this are of little consequence. Whether the program is intelligent or merely simulates intelligence, for example, matters little as long as it carries out its task. And if the program makes available, in the form of expertise or know-how, a resource that would otherwise be scarce, then AI has surely made some worthwhile contribution.

From AI to expert systems

Artificial intelligence's aim of studying the underlying principles of mental organization can be seen as stemming from a long-held view that thinking *is* in some way the logical manipulation of symbols. To this extent, it matters little that the manipulation is performed by a brain or a computer because it is the manipulation that is important and not the medium. Early work in AI concentrated on the activity of problem-solving. To exhibit intelligent behaviour can be seen as solving a problem not just in the sense of solving artificial problems, as in an examination, but in coping successfully with the situations that need to be faced in order to manage in any environment. The search for general methods of solving problems, a part of what is referred to because of the generality of its aim as *weak AI*, proved elusive, at least in terms of producing general methods capable of solving difficult problems. The major positive conclusion of the work was that hard problems could only be solved with the aid of knowledge about the problem domain.

The application of these ideas led to the development of what are known as *knowledge-based systems*. These systems attempt to solve problems by using relevant knowledge and techniques of AI but not necessarily with any claim to do so in the same way as humans might.

Knowledge-based systems occupy an intermediate position between the original weak AI systems and expert systems which, in contrast, are called 'strong' in deference to the fact that they operate in a very restricted

Introduction

domain and make use of highly specific knowledge of that domain. In the light of this chain of development, an expert system can be defined as a knowledge-based system that makes use of knowledge obtained from an expert so as to emulate the competence of that expert within a well-defined field of application.

Thus, the thread of development leading to expert systems displays a movement from broad to tightly restrained areas of application, from seeking to explain mental organization to seeking to create engineering artifacts and from widely applicable methods to those that are quite specific.

The trend from general methods to those that are specific to a particular domain has, though, been reversed to some extent. It has been observed that many tasks have common requirements. This has led to the creation of systems capable of satisfying these requirements in the form of expert system *shells*. A shell is an expert system from which the knowledge has been 'emptied', so that the new knowledge required for a particular task can be 'poured in' to replace it. Expert system shells are now available for use on microcomputers and almost any other type of computer.

What is an expert system and why is it needed?

An expert system is, from the point of view of its users, a computer program to be used in the same way as any other. But from the point of view of its designers and implementors an expert system is quite different from a conventional computer program. For one thing, it incorporates a knowledge base, containing the knowledge it needs, and it operates by manipulating that knowledge in some formal manner. Secondly, conventional programs are written in a computer language such as *C* or *Fortran*, and they describe to the computer in every detail how it is to go about a task. Expert systems can also be written in these languages, and some have been, but *Lisp* or *Prolog* are more usual choices. They are used because they are more suitable for manipulating the structures with which knowledge is represented, and because they support a different style of programming in which the resulting programs are descriptive rather than prescriptive. That is to say, they describe what the computer is to do, and then, in some sense, leave the computer to decide how to do it rather than spelling out exactly how the computer is to perform its task. The resulting programs are much more likely to be free of errors and are also more amenable to change.

The reason that expert systems are needed can be illustrated by relating the way in which one of them came to exist. *R1* is the name of an expert system used by Digital Equipment Corporation (DEC) to configure some of its computer systems, including its VAXs. It is one of the most successful of all expert systems and has saved DEC large amounts of money.

The initial impetus for *R1*'s development stemmed from the fact that DEC does not offer ready-made systems, but expects its customers to specify their own systems from the units that it does make. The company decided to try to develop a program to check customers' orders for consistency and then to plan the way in which the system would be assembled into cabinets so that, when delivered, it would fit into the accommodation reserved for it. All attempts to write a conventional program to do this failed, and it was only when a knowledge-based approach was adopted that *R1* emerged as a successful means of performing the required activities.

The essence of the reasons for the failure of the conventional approach was the difficulty, if not impossibility, of anticipating in advance all the possible configurations that might be ordered, as well as the ways in which they might be packaged, so that the instructions for dealing with each situation could be written. The number of ways of selecting a system as a combination of units drawn from a large range of possibilities suffered from the well-known effects of the combinatorial explosion. The regular addition of new units and the withdrawal of existing ones only served to complicate matters further.

But with the adoption of a knowledge-based approach, it was possible to proceed by recording knowledge of the attributes of each unit, of the ways that units could be interconnected and how they could be packaged. This knowledge could then be manipulated to determine whether a particular combination of units comprised a complete system and, if it did, further knowledge could be invoked to determine a configuration for the system that satisfied the constraints imposed by the requirements of the customer.

Changes to the product line require only that the corresponding changes be made to the knowledge base. The system for manipulating the knowledge need not be altered at all. The essence of the success of the knowledge-based approach, not only in this case but also in others, is that it is more effective to manipulate knowledge of the problem domain explicitly (after placing it in a knowledge base) than to do so implicitly by embedding it in many and various procedures.

(How *R1* is supposed to have come by its name is too unlikely not to retell. The story is that one of its implementors was heard to say: 'Eighteen

Introduction

months ago I'd never heard the term *knowledge engineer*, and now I are one.')

Activity

Compile a list of intelligent activities that an expert system might be able to do for you. Are there any such activities that you would object to a computer taking over?

Areas of application and their characteristics

Medicine is a fruitful application area for expert systems: some medical expert systems that we shall meet again are *MYCIN, PIP* and *CASNET.* Their functions are, respectively:

- to diagnose a range of infectious diseases and to recommend appropriate treatments
- to diagnose the state of kidney disease in a patient by assessing the progress of its development
- to manage the treatment of diseases the development of which is well understood.

These are all, in fact, examples of a wider range of systems referred to variously as *advice-giving systems* and *intelligent advisors*. Their forte is diagnosis and treatment recommendation, and such systems are widely used in the management of complex systems as well as in the management of patients. A number have been developed to locate and correct faults occurring in complex electronic systems and in communications networks.

Many advice-giving systems must deal with situations in which complete information is not available. Just as a doctor all too often has to make a judgement without a perfect knowledge of a patient's symptoms or despite the fact that a disease is imperfectly understood, so expert systems must operate in the same circumstances. The ability of expert systems to deal with uncertainty is just one of their contributions to computer science.

Expert systems are also used as part of the decision mechanisms which control directly some aspects of the operation of, among others, defence systems, communication networks and power stations. Their use in defence is both controversial and secret, but they have also been used in applications as diverse as communications receiving equipment and systems for the automatic management of the operation of telephone networks. It has been demonstrated that by applying knowledge to the control of complex operations, expert systems can help achieve performance levels at least as high as those obtained with conventional control mechanisms.

The activities for which expert systems have been, and could be, developed share a number of characteristics. First, they should be medium-sized, in the sense of not being trivial while not being extremely complicated.

Second, and most important, there should be no precisely defined way of performing the activity (that is, there should be no algorithm for it), for then a conventional computer program can be written. It should be the sort of activity that is carried out with the aid of rules of thumb (or heuristics) which have the property that they help towards the achievement of the activity in certain circumstances but not in others. This implies that knowledge of how to go about the activity is available from some source, perhaps from a person who is an expert at the activity or perhaps by finding it in text books, manuals and documents. If we think in terms of a human expert, then the person concerned must be willing and able to reveal his or her expertise. It may be possible to build an expert system that outperforms any single human expert by incorporating knowledge from more than one expert but, if this is done, care must be taken to ensure that the knowledge from different experts is complementary, perhaps providing alternative ways of doing certain things, and is not contradictory.

Third, to have any real value once it has been constructed, an expert system must show a satisfactory level of performance in terms of both the speed at which it runs and its reliability. It will only inspire confidence in its users if it can explain and justify the solutions and recommendations it produces.

Fourth, it ought to be able to accommodate new knowledge by adding it to its existing knowledge base with a minimum of difficulty so that it can cope with changes to the environment housing its activity or to new discoveries in its area of expertise.

Lastly, it should be able to communicate its stored knowledge in a form that is easy to comprehend: in this way, the knowledge can be checked, inspected or used as a basis for training and education.

Introduction

Activity
From the relevant journals and books in your library, compile a list of three or four applications of expert systems. Briefly outline the role of the expert system in each case. Can you detect characteristics that any of the application areas have in common?

Other related subjects

It is probably clear already that the creation of an expert system is an activity that crosses traditional subject boundaries. A knowledge of computer science is needed to create the program for the expert system and to decide on the appropriate hardware to run it. An appreciation of the needs of the user and of the ways in which the program can be made natural to use is also needed. The so-called human–computer interface is an area that is studied in its own right, and it draws on ideas from psychology. Then again, with an expert system for use in medicine, some familiarity with medicine is needed to appreciate and acquire the requisite medical knowledge for the system, while familiarity with medical practice is needed to accommodate the needs of the medical practitioners who will use the system.

Knowledge itself has also been a subject of study: the branch of philosophy known as epistemology is the study of the theory of knowledge. (Expressed more informally, it is the study of what we know about what we know. This apparent circularity or, more accurately, self reference, is characteristic of our whole area. In studying intelligence, for instance, we are using our intelligence to try and understand our intelligence.) To the extent that the builder of an expert system is dealing with knowledge, it would be foolish to neglect altogether the results of centuries of thinking about knowledge.

In the same vein, cognitive science, which is broadly the study of entities capable of sensation, perception and cognition, is another subject of relevance. The subject draws on many others, including philosophy, psychology, linguistics and anthropology. More recently, it has interacted with AI, which has provided it with many computational metaphors for processes that were previously less well defined, even to the extent that it can be approached through computer science quite as well as through a more traditional area such as, for example, experimental psychology.

The main point is that many areas have a contribution to make to expert systems. Those with an awareness only of the computer-related aspects may be able to create an expert system, but they are unlikely to produce one that is either worth using or capable of providing any insight into its area of application. In fact, an expert system is likely to be created by a team whose members possess a range of inter-disciplinary and multi-disciplinary skills.

Assignment 1

In your role as Head of Research, you have been asked to produce a report to help the Chief Administrator of your hospital assess the possibility of introducing expert systems to help relieve the pressure of work on the medical staff. Your report should be about two pages long. It should discuss the feasibility, likely effectiveness and practicality of such a course of action. It should mention any other ways other than diagnosis in which the systems could help doctors. It should also consider the likely response of the doctors.

Recap

- the aim of artificial intelligence is to make computers do the kinds of things that are generally considered to require intelligence when done by people
- knowledge is the key to intelligent behaviour
- the failure of AI to produce methods of solving problems that are applicable in any circumstances led to the examination of problem-solving in less general domains and eventually to expert systems which operate successfully in narrow and quite specific areas of application
- expert systems are the first useful products to result from the pursuit of AI
- an expert system is a system that makes use of knowledge obtained from an expert to emulate the competence of that expert within a well-defined field of application
- expert systems bring knowledge about how to perform a task to bear in the course of performing it, rather than following procedures specifying how to cope with every possible variation on the task
- the creation of expert systems draws on many other subjects including computer science, psychology and cognitive science. Knowledge, and other matters of relevance, are long-established subjects of study, and the results of these studies are available to help contribute towards the development of expert systems.

2: The principles of operation of expert systems

Objectives

After reading this chapter, you should be able to:
- explain what a state transition system is
- understand how a state transition system can model the activities required of an expert system
- appreciate the need for backtracking
- follow the procedure for carrying out backtracking
- justify a general structure applicable to all expert systems.

Scenario

The programmer confronts his project supervisor in the open-plan office of the software house.

'Look, I've only ever written conventional programs. I've no idea even how to start working on this expert system for you.'

'I see. You certainly can't think about it in the same way as one of your usual programming jobs.'

'I know that. But how *do* I think about it?'

The purpose of this chapter is to introduce and explain the basic ideas underlying the operation of expert systems. When examined in detail, different expert systems have different structures and modes of operation but, in broad terms, there are some common principles.

A number of specific applications are used as a basis for this attempt to expose and discuss these principles. To avoid giving the impression that the principles are linked to a specific application, the same model is used

Advanced Students' Guide to Expert Systems

for each application so that it can easily be seen that they emerge from the common approach and not from the specific example. The model is the state transition diagram, and it is described in the next section.

State transition model

An activity can be described in terms of its component events. At any time while the activity is in progress, an event may have occurred, may be happening or may be waiting to occur. The situation at any time may be described in terms of the status of the events involved in the activity. A state transition diagram such as the one in Figure 2.1, consists of circles (more usually called nodes) joined by arrows (or arcs). It provides an abstract model by means of which an activity can be described and examined, because its nodes can be used to represent the states of the activity, and the arcs to represent the ways in which one state is succeeded by another. The labels on the arcs indicate the action that causes the progression from the state at the tail of the arrow to that at the tip. Figure 2.1 shows the various states that are possible during the activity of climbing a flight of three stairs when the only actions that are possible are taking one step up the stairs and taking one step down. The activity usually starts at the bottom of the stairs, and is completed by reaching the top.

The set of states in a state transition diagram is referred to as the *state space*. The state space of Figure 2.1, for example, contains four states.

Figure 2.2 shows a completely abstract state transition diagram. It can be interpreted as describing an activity in just the same way as Figure 2.1, but it is also possible to see it as describing the set of rules that govern the progress of the activity. The rules are:

- if the system is in state 1 and action A is taken
  then the system moves to state 2

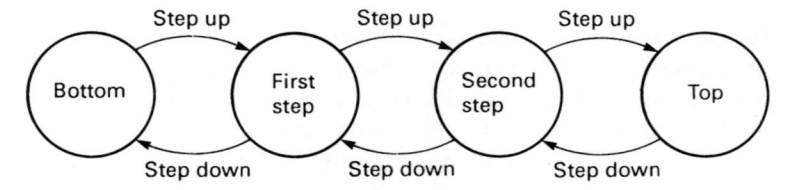

Figure 2.1 *A state transition diagram*

The principles of operation of expert systems

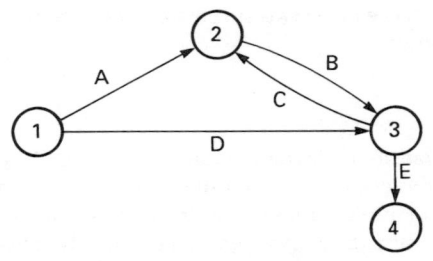

Figure 2.2 *An abstract state transition diagram*

- if the system is in state 1 and action D is taken then the system moves to state 3

and so on.

These rules can be written in the following way:

- if state = 1 and action A then state = 2
- if state = 1 and action D then state = 3

and so on.

Question 1

Express the state transition diagram of Figure 2.1 as a set of rules.

Question 2

Convert the following set of rules to a state transition diagram:

  IF state = 0 and COIN = 5p THEN state = 1
  IF state = 0 and COIN = 10p THEN state = 2
  IF state = 1 and COIN = 5p THEN state = 2
  IF state = 1 and COIN = 10p THEN (state = 3; action3; state = 2)
  IF state = i and (COIN < 5p or COIN > 10p) THEN (state = 4; action4; state = i).

What would action3 and action4 consist of?

Question 3

Draw a state transition diagram for the game of tennis. The state of the game can be represented by the score at the end of a point. The starting state is

13

Advanced Students' Guide to Expert Systems

'0–0'. Each state has exactly two successors since the server either wins or loses the next point.

Question 4

Draw the state transition diagram for an imaginary unit as failures occur to take it towards the end of its useful life. The unit contains three identical sub-units. If one of the sub-units works, the unit itself works properly. When the current sub-unit fails, another unit automatically replaces it. (Hint: the state can be represented by, say, (W, F, W) to indicate that sub-units 1 and 3 work, and sub-unit 2 has failed.)

Expert system models

This section gives four examples of the ways that a state transition diagram provides a model for activities of the kind required of expert systems.

Planning actions

A way of making a plan to carry out a specific task can be demonstrated in the context of the simple blocks world that consists of nothing more than a number of blocks on a table and an arm that is capable of picking up a block and putting it down again. A task consists of rearranging the blocks, so that an initial configuration is changed to some other specified configuration. A plan will be a sequence of actions which, when followed by the arm, will achieve the task.

In the blocks world, a block can either be on the table or on another block. The arm can lift only a single block, so that it can only pick up a block that is on the table with nothing on it, or is on the top of a pile of blocks. We can begin by considering the blocks world in which there are only two blocks, labelled A and B. There are only three distinguishable states of this microworld. They are:

1   block A and B are both on the table
2   block A is on block B
3   block B is on block A.

These states are shown in Figure 2.3. It is not hard to see that state 1 is changed to state 2 by picking up block A and putting it on block B. Similar pairs of actions cause a change from one state to another as shown in Figure 2.3: the transitions are labelled with the actions necessary to cause

The principles of operation of expert systems

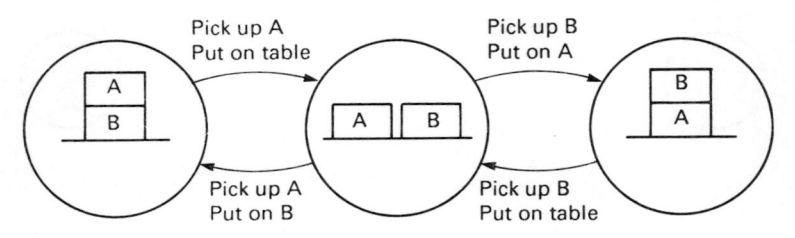

Figure 2.3 *State transition diagram for a small blocks world*

the corresponding change. In this way, all the states that can occur in this microworld and the ways in which one state can be changed to another are represented by a state transition diagram.

Now, to plan a way of carrying out the task of changing one state of the world to another, all that is necessary is to find a path from the one to the other, and to read off the instructions on each arc along the path. Let us try this for the task of changing the situation in which block A is on block B, so that state 2 is the initial state, to that in which block B is on block A, so that the goal is to achieve state 3. Starting from state 2, the only transition is to state 1. There is a choice of transitions from this node, and it is possible to go back to state 2 as shown in Figure 2.4. In fact, the search for a path could follow this loop for ever, never finding the path to state 3. For this reason, it is a good idea to change from simply searching for a path to finding a path that does not visit the same state more than once. With this strategy, the search moves from the initial state to state 1 as before, but then the next transitions can be considered, and the move back to the initial state ruled out so that the search arrives at the goal state in two moves, as shown in Figure 2.5. Reading the instructions from this path gives the plan of action as:

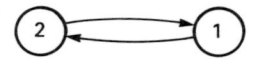

Figure 2.4 *Transitions in the blocks world*

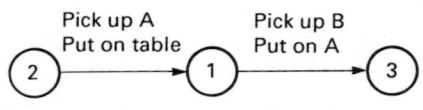

Figure 2.5 *The transitions that carry out the task*

Advanced Students' Guide to Expert Systems

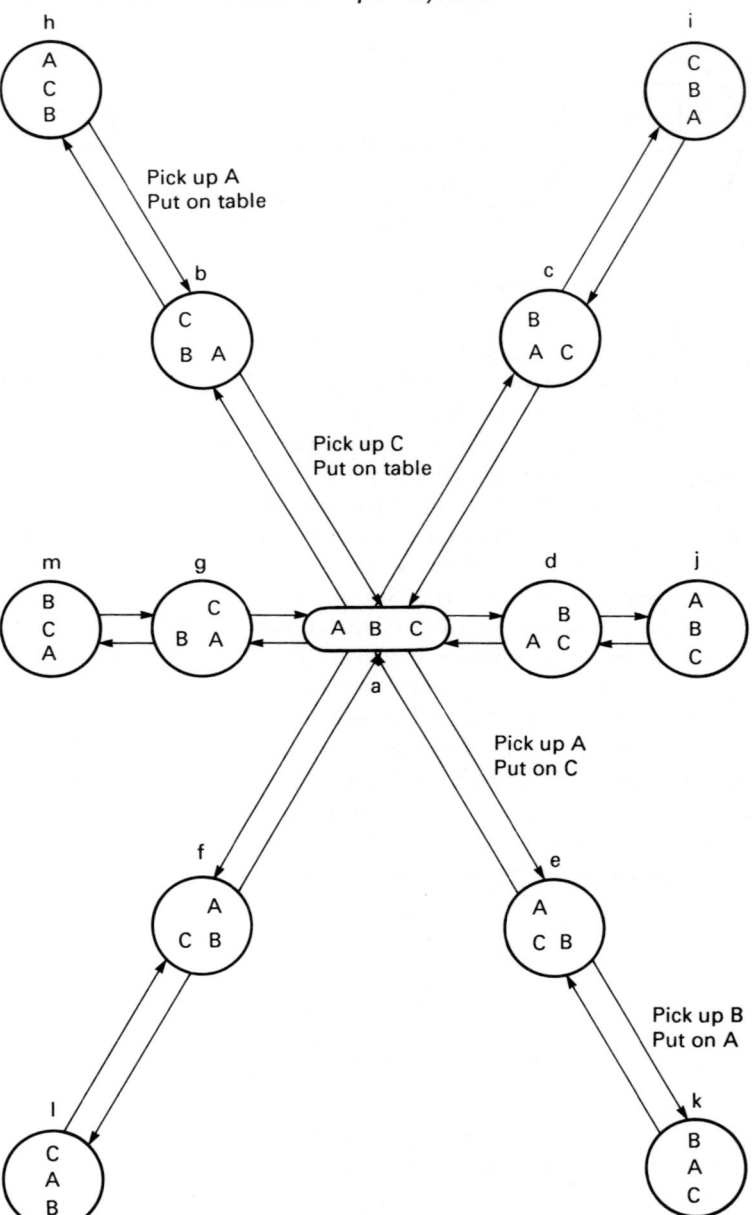

Figure 2.6 State transition diagram for the blocks world with three blocks

The principles of operation of expert systems

- state 2 to state 1 – pick up A; put it on the table
- state 1 to state 3 – pick up B; put it on A.

This very simple situation illustrates the method by which a plan to accomplish a task may be made, but it may well be too simple to be convincing. For this reason, we turn to the blocks world in which there are three blocks. This world has a state in which all three blocks are on the table, six states in which there is a pile of two blocks and six more with all three blocks in one pile. The states are shown in Figure 2.6 with all the transitions corresponding to the 'pick up – put down' actions that transform one state to another. The illustration is redrawn as Figure 2.7, with the states identified by letters rather than patterns of blocks, for ease of reference in what follows.

Consider the task of moving from the situation in which block B is on the table with block C on it and block A on top of C, to that in which block C is on the table with block A on it and block B on top of A. That is, the initial state is *h* and the goal state is *k*. From state *h*, the only transition is

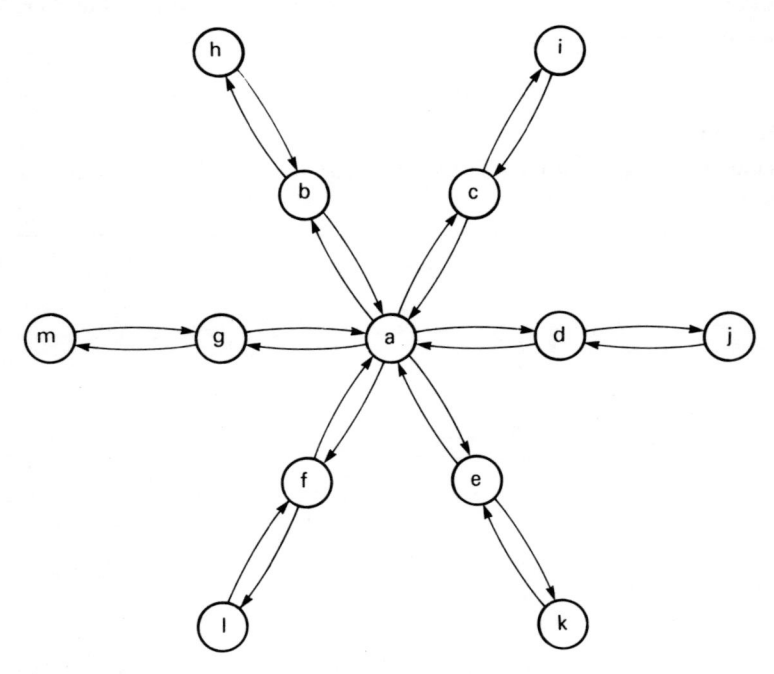

Figure 2.7 *An alternative representation of Figure 2.6*

17

Advanced Students' Guide to Expert Systems

to *b*, but then there are two alternatives, both of which are valid. Let us make the search proceed by choosing the possible transitions in clockwise order from the point at which the node is entered. This develops the path *h, b, a, c, i* at which point progress comes to a halt because the only transition from *i* leads back to *c* which has been visited already. But all is not lost because there are other paths from *c* so, writing off *i*, the search backtracks to *c* and becomes *h, b, a, c, d, j* before hitting the dead end at *j*. Now *j* is discarded and the search backtracks to *d*, but the only other paths from there lead to *a* and *c*, both of which have been visited previously, so *c* must be discarded. This causes backtracking to *a*, from where the path *h, b, a* can continue as *h, b, a, e, k* and so reach the goal. Phew! All this is summarized in Figure 2.8, where the dotted line indicates the way that the search backtracks when it hits a dead end.

In fact, it is possible for the search to backtrack even when the goal state has been reached, and it can be worth doing so because there may be alternative ways of achieving the task, and some of them may be better than the first one found by the search. In this case, we have found the shortest path and, correspondingly the best way to do the task, but there are other ways to do it.

Question 5

How many states are there in the state space of a blocks world with four blocks?

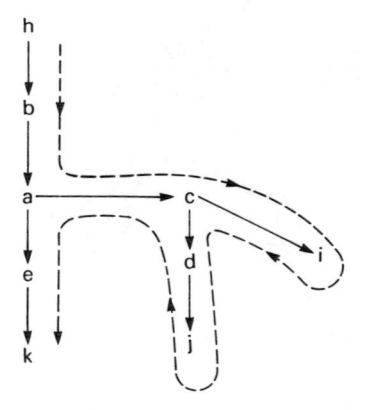

Figure 2.8 *Finding the path to the goal state*

The principles of operation of expert systems

Solving a problem

Now let us see how to use the state transition diagram to solve a problem. A farmer is on the bank of a river with a wolf, a goat, and a cabbage. There is a boat which he can row, but he cannot take more than one passenger with him. He has to get all of them to the other side of the river. The trouble is that the wolf will eat the goat if the farmer ever leaves them together, and the goat will eat the cabbage if he leaves them.

The first thing to decide is how to represent the state of the problem. The initial situation has all four participants on one bank (the east bank, say) and the problem is solved when they all arrive safely on the other bank (the west one). This suggests that the state can be captured by recording the bank on which each participant is located. In this way, the state of affairs at any time can be written as:

(F, W, G, C)

where F denotes the position of the farmer, W that of the wolf, G that of the goat and C that of the cabbage. Each of the four components of a state can take on the value e or w to indicate that the corresponding participant is on, respectively, the east or the west bank. Now the problem begins in the state (e, e, e, e) and the goal is to reach the state (w, w, w, w), so the computer can be told to solve the problem by finding a path from the initial state to the goal state which does not visit any state more than once.

Actually, this is not quite good enough, because the path might include, for example, the state (e, w, w, e). This means that the farmer and the cabbage are on the east bank while the wolf and the goat are on the west. But if the farmer leaves the wolf and the goat together, the goat will be eaten, after which there is no way that all four can finish up on the west bank! The state (e, e, w, w) is one of a number of others that prevent a satisfactory conclusion to the problem (why?). The point is that some states are what we might call 'unsafe', and in view of this the computer ought to be told to find a path from the initial state to the goal state that does not visit any state more than once and does not include any unsafe states.

Now, the process of finding a path can proceed by trying in turn all the states that can be reached from the initial state, and testing them to see if they are safe. If a state is found to which it is safe to proceed, the path to it can be followed, and the procedure repeated from there. The next states can be generated by finding in turn the states that result from the farmer rowing across the river by himself, or by rowing across with any one of the

Advanced Students' Guide to Expert Systems

participants on the same bank as him. From the initial state, the farmer can cross alone, cross with the wolf, with the goat or with the cabbage. These next states can be generated by, respectively, changing the first component of the state description from e to w (or, more generally, changing them from e to w or from w to e as necessary); changing the first and second components; changing the first and third components; and changing the first and fourth components. The successors of (e, e, e, e) are, as shown in Figure 2.9, (w, e, e, e), (w, w, e, e), (w, e, w, e) and (w, e, e, w). Of these, only the third is safe, and so it must be the first state on the path towards the goal state. The only possible successors of (w, e, w, e) are (e, e, w, e) and (e, e, e, e) corresponding to the farmer rowing back alone and rowing back with the goat. The first state is safe: the second restores the initial situation and, as a second visit to that state, is ruled out. Thus the next state is (e, e, w, e). This and the ensuing states that complete a path to the goal state are shown in Figure 2.10. The complete solution path, with the sequence of moves it represents, is:

(e, e, e, e); the initial state
(w, e, w, e); the farmer rows the goat across
(e, e, w, e); the farmer rows back alone
(w, w, w, e); the farmer rows the wolf across
(e, w, e, e); the farmer rows back with the goat
(w, w, e, w); the farmer rows the cabbage across
(e, w, e, w); the farmer rows back
(w, w, w, w); the farmer rows the goat across to reach the goal.

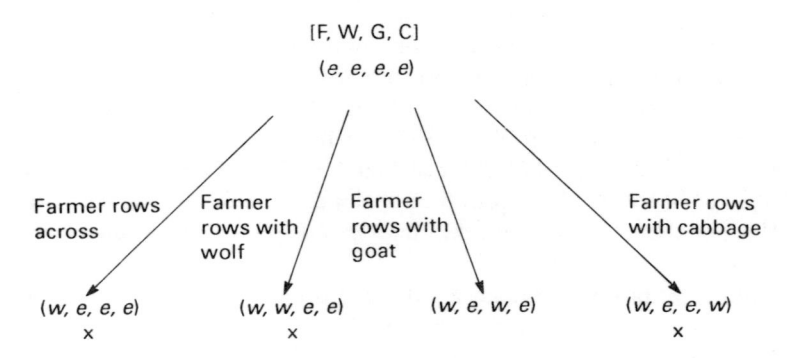

Figure 2.9 Finding the first move

The principles of operation of expert systems

```
                            (e, e, e, e)
              ╱           ╱       │        ╲
      (w, e, e, e)  (w, w, e, e)  (w, e, w, e)  (w, e, e, w)
          x            x              │            x
                                      ▼
                                 (e, e, w, e) ────── (e, e, e, e)
                              ╱       │       ╲
                    (w, e, w, e)  (w, w, w, e)  (w, e, w, w)
                          ╱          │              ╲
               (e, w, w, e)    (e, e, w, e)      (e, w, e, e)
                    x                                  │
                          ╱          │              ╱
               (w, w, e, e)    (w, w, w, e)    (w, w, e, w)
                          ╲          │              │
               (e, w, e, w)    (e, w, e, e)    (e, e, e, w)
                    ╱                │
      (w, w, e, w)            (w, w, w, w)
                                  GOAL
```

x unsafe state
— repeated state

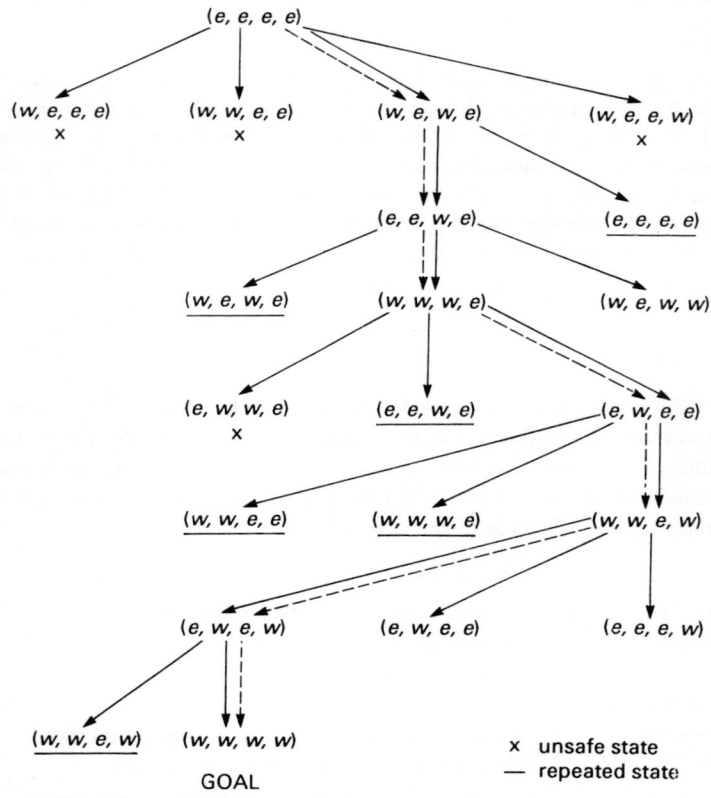

Figure 2.10 *The path to the goal state*

This path is found first as a consequence of the order in which the next states are generated. There may be others, as the successor states of (w, e, w, w) in the fourth row of Figure 2.10 have not been explored. If there is a shorter path, that is, a path of fewer states, it is a better solution in the sense that the farmer has to row across the river less often, and so expend less energy, in order to achieve the same result.

Activity

Check the states in Figure 2.10 to be sure that you know why each is safe or unsafe.

21

Advanced Students' Guide to Expert Systems

Question 6
Solve the following problem. Three missionaries and three cannibals are all at a river crossing where there is a boat with room only for two people. They all want to cross the river. But if there are ever more cannibals than missionaries on a bank, the cannibals will eat the missionaries. The problem is to find a way to get everyone across safely. (Hint: a good description for the state is, for example, (2, 3, w) to indicate that there are two cannibals and three missionaries still to cross, and the boat is on the west bank.)

Diagnosis

Suppose that a school doctor has made the following table to show the symptoms of the diseases most commonly suffered by the pupils in his school. (The table has been made up for the purposes of this book. It should not be taken seriously as a medical aid, and should certainly not be used in place of a visit to the doctor!)

Illness	Symptoms
glandular fever	lethargy, headache, high temperature
measles	lethargy, high temperature, spots
asthma	breathing difficulty
common cold	sore throat, runny nose
bronchitis	coughing, breathing difficulty, high temperature
'flu	headache, sore throat, high temperature
tonsillitis	sore throat

A state transition diagram based on this table is shown in Figure 2.11. The initial state represents the beginning of the diagnostic session before any of the patient's symptoms have been made known to the system. A symptom causes the transition to a successor state which, as a collection of one or more symptoms, represents a partial diagnosis. Each path in the diagram terminates at a state corresponding to a complete diagnosis, so that there are seven goal states.

To illustrate, entering the symptom *sore throat* at the initial state drives the system to the state we might call 'sore throat only', from where the entry of *headache* drives it to the state 'sore throat and headache only' and then *high temperature* causes the immediate transition to the state giving the diagnosis of *'flu*. The transition to the state giving the diagnosis *tonsillitis* corresponds to the set of symptoms consisting of 'sore throat

The principles of operation of expert systems

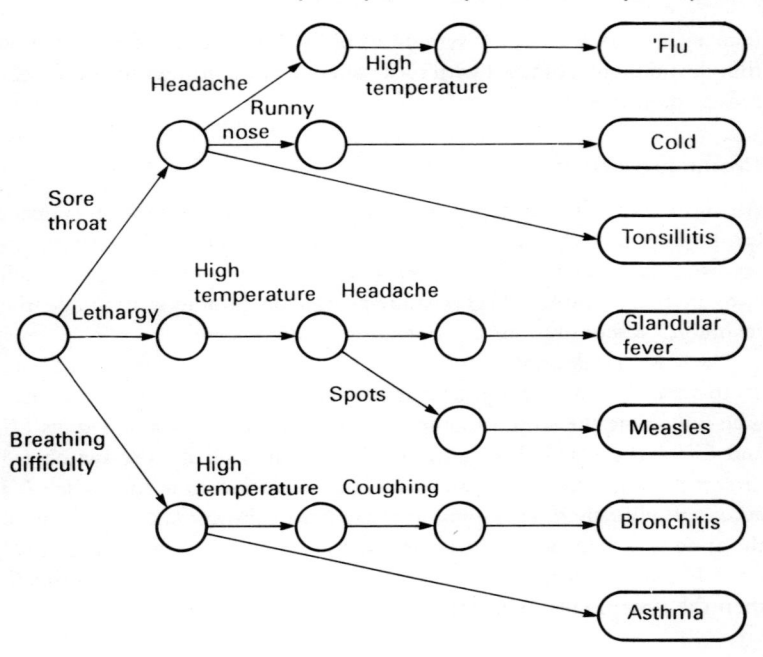

Figure 2.11 *State transition diagram for diagnosing illnesses*

only', so that this transition can occur only when the patient has a sore throat but not a headache and not a runny nose (that is, the patient does not have the two symptoms that cause transitions from the 'sore throat only' state). To put this in another way, it is not the case that every patient with either 'flu or a cold also has tonsillitis: the absence of symptoms is as significant as their presence.

The state transition diagram can also be seen to correspond to a dialogue between doctor and patient. The doctor can begin by asking the patient: 'Is your throat sore?' If the answer is 'Yes', the next question should be: 'Have you got a headache?' while if it is 'No' the succeeding question is: 'Do you feel lethargic?' The diagram gives the complete structure for the dialogues needed to diagnose each and every illness that patients can suffer in the tidy world where only these seven illnesses occur.

It may be noted that the diagram can also be used to decide whether a doctor's hunch about the illness suffered by a patient is correct. By moving from the state corresponding to the diagnosis to the initial state

Advanced Students' Guide to Expert Systems

(and against the arrows) the symptoms of the hypothesised disease can be found, and then compared with those offered by the patient to confirm or refute the diagnosis.

Producing advice

As a fourth and final example, we consider how a state transition diagram can be built to keep track of the status of a system in which components are liable to fail and need to be replaced. By attaching a message to each state in the transition diagram, advice can be produced to guide the technician responsible for the operation of the system.

The system is illustrated in Figure 2.12. It has two units, labelled U and V, in parallel, and both must be active for the system to be operational. The units have the same structure: U contains the identical sub-units $U1$ and $U2$, and the switch $U3$; while V is similar. Initially, the switch $U3$ directs the input to the system to $U1$, but if $U1$ fails then the switch $U3$ automatically switches the input to the standby sub-unit $U2$. V operates in the same way. The point is that the system can withstand the failure of $U1$ or of $V1$, and even the failure of $U1$ and $V1$. But if $U1$ and $U2$ both fail, then the system fails, as it does if $V1$ and $V2$ fail.

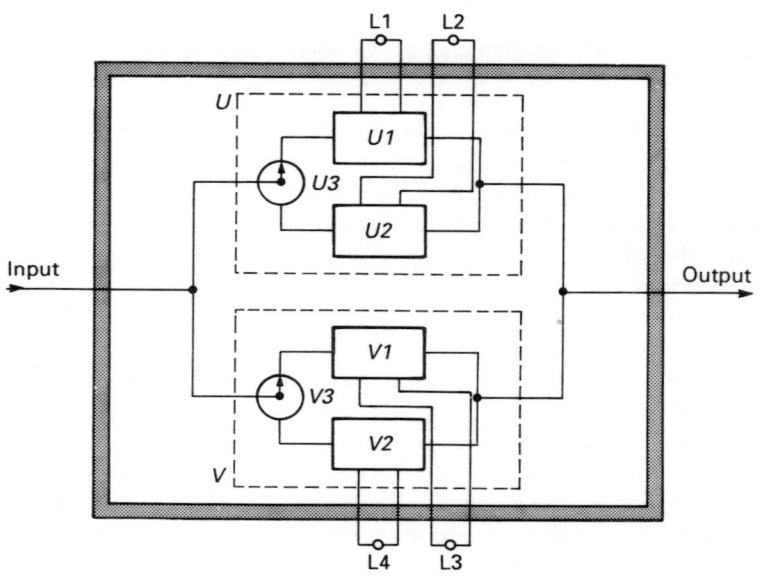

Figure 2.12 The system

The principles of operation of expert systems

There is a light associated with each sub-unit which comes on if, and only if, the sub-unit is active. In this way, the status of the system is indicated by the on-off pattern of the four lights. So, initially, the pattern of lights is:

light for $U1$ (L1) is on,
light for $U2$ (L2) is off,
light for $V1$ (L3) is on,
light for $V2$ (L4) is off,

This suggests that the state description should consist of the state of each of the four lights L1 to L4, so that the initial state takes the form (on, off, on, off). From here, a transition to another state occurs when a unit fails: the failure of $U1$ leads to (off, on, on, off) and the failure of $V1$ to (on, off, off, on). Neither of these states prevents the system from operating, but their occurrence should produce a message advising the technician to replace the faulty unit and to reset the switch to return the system to its initial state. The advice may be ignored, and in each case a further failure can occur, to give the state (off, on, off, on), without stopping the system from operating. But if $U2$ fails after $U1$, then the system fails, and the technician must be advised to replace both sub-units as a matter of urgency. It is not necessary to trace the effect of further failures because at this point the system has failed and there is no way that things can get any worse.

The state transition diagram developed to the points of overall system failure is shown in Figure 2.13. Each state is tagged with the appropriate advice to the technician. In fact, the advice message could just as easily be made a fifth component of the state description.

Reviewing the situation

The examples of the previous section show that some cleverer things that people do can be achieved with the aid of a basically quite simple process. As that process can be described, it can be carried out by a computer. In this way, a computer can be made to exhibit intelligent behaviour. There is no claim that the computer is being intelligent. In fact, since the basis of its behaviour is a more or less mechanical search, it might be considered quite unintelligent. But it can simulate intelligent behaviour and, when judged by its behaviour (as opposed to the mechanism producing its behaviour), it can appear intelligent.

For the purpose of explanation, the examples are necessarily of a small scale, but it should not be hard to imagine that their scale can be increased.

Advanced Students' Guide to Expert Systems

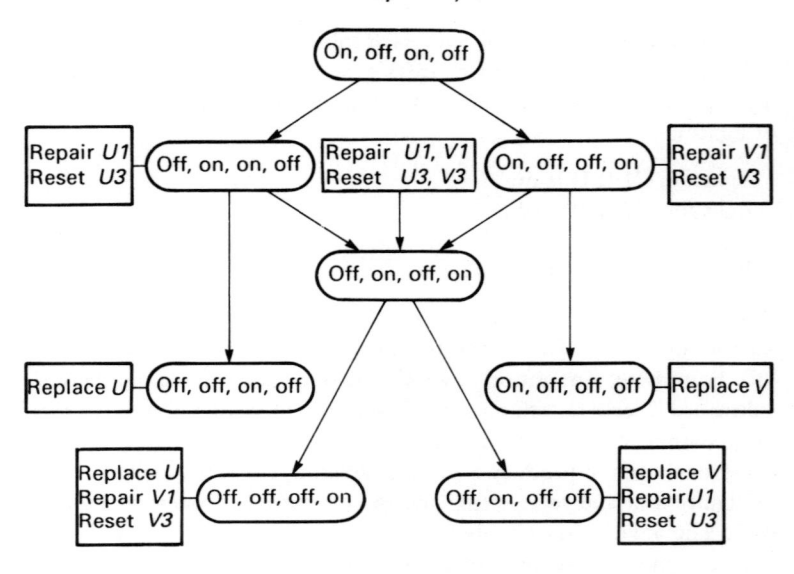

Figure 2.13 State transition diagram for diagnosing system faults

Problems do occur, though, with very large state spaces, for then the search procedure may not be able to explore the state space in a reasonable time. This leaves medium-sized state spaces, between the small 'toy' ones and those that are too time-consuming to explore, as the province of worthwhile expert systems.

In the examples, the states of different state spaces are used to characterize the status of the environment of an activity, a problem, the application of expertise and the operation of a system. Paths in these state spaces represent the various paths that may be followed as a result of the occurrence of events in these environments. The aim in each case is to find a way of achieving some objective such as performing a task or solving a problem. Discovering the process by which it may be achieved corresponds to finding a path from a given initial state to a goal state.

The construction of a state space begins by finding a way of describing the states. This is not necessarily easy, and requires some experience before it can be done consistently with success. A good description should catch the essence of the situation and yet be compact. In the problem of the farmer, the wolf and the goat, for example, the *positions* of the four participants are all that really matters. A boat is involved in the problem

The principles of operation of expert systems

but, as the farmer is the only one who can row it, the boat must always be where the farmer is and so there is no need to mention it at all. The system of Figure 2.12 may be described at several levels: as one system, two units or four sub-units. Again the sub-units themselves may contain many components, and a description could be composed in terms of them or even, at a deeper level, in terms of the atoms and electrons inside them. The level of description that is appropriate in terms of producing advice for a technician attending the system is the sub-unit level, and the only aspect of a sub-unit that is relevant is whether it is currently operating. In this way, the appropriate state description need only record whether each sub-unit is operating.

The point is that the state description affects all that follows: with a good description the state space will be compact while with a bad one it will sprawl and contain redundancy. Some of the early successes of artificial intelligence were first taken to show the power of search, but have subsequently been recognized to owe as much to apt descriptions.

Given a state description, the transitions between states, and with them the structure of the state space, follow from the application. The state space can then be explored by a process of search. The search can be mechanical and systematic, but we have seen that it needs some guidance. The guidance is supplied in the form of knowledge. Looping is prevented by the common-sense idea of avoiding a state if it has been visited before, and this sort of knowledge applies equally to any application. That certain states are unsafe and so should be avoided in the farmer, wolf, goat and cabbage problem is knowledge that is specific to that problem. It helps in that application, but not in any other. As the size of the state space increases so the use of local knowledge becomes more important. Exhaustive exploration becomes more time consuming in large spaces: to be effective, the search must be confined to the more relevant parts of the space.

We have also seen that the search procedure must be able to backtrack, not only so that it can recover when it finds itself at a dead end from which no further progress is possible but also to be able to find alternative solutions that may be better than the first one it comes across.

Figure 2.8 illustrates the result of backtracking, but does not explain how it may be done. To complete the coverage of the search process at the level of this chapter, a mechanism for backtracking is presented in the next section. Then, in the final section, all the aspects discussed in this section are drawn together to give a general structure for an expert system.

27

Advanced Students' Guide to Expert Systems

How to backtrack

The following procedure achieves backtracking when exploring a state space that has no closed paths (that is to say, loops) in it, such as that of Figure 2.11. It can be generalized so that it works for state spaces that do contain loops, but this complicates it somewhat. The procedure makes use of two lists: one named *WAITING* is for states that are awaiting examination and the second, named *DONE*, is for those that have been examined. The successors of a state are the states to which it is linked directly by transitions. The procedure is:

- initialization
    WAITING is the list containing just the initial state
    DONE is empty
- repeat
    remove the first state from *WAITING*
    find its successors and put them at the beginning of *WAITING*
    put the state from *WAITING* at the beginning of *DONE*
- until
    WAITING is empty (the search fails)
    or the goal state is on the end of *DONE* (the search path is in *DONE*)

The procedure can be illustrated using the state space of Figure 2.14, where the initial state is *a* and the goal is, say, *f* by recording the successive contents of *WAITING* and *DONE*.

	WAITING	DONE
Initially:	[*a*]	[]

The successors of *a* are *b* and *c*
    [*b, c*]   [*a*]
The successors of *b* are *d* and *e*
    [*d, e, c*]   [*a, b*]
d has no successors
    [*e, c*]   [*a, b, d*]
The search backtracks through *b* to *e*. It has no successors
    [*c*]   [*a, b, d, e*]
The search backtracks through *b* and *a* to *c*. The successors of *c* are *f* and *g*
    [*f, g*]   [*a, b, d, e, c*]
f has no successors
    [*g*]   [*a, b, d, e, c, f*]

The principles of operation of expert systems

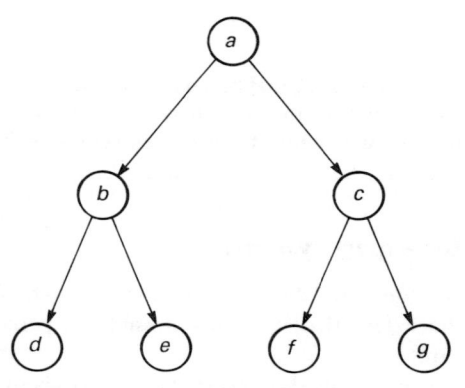

Figure 2.14 *A state space to be searched*

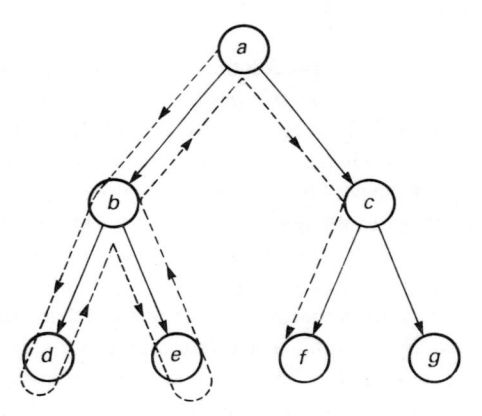

Figure 2.15 *The path followed by backtracking in reaching f*

Now the goal state, *f*, is at the end of *DONE*. The search has succeeded and the search path is in *DONE*.

The path is marked on Figure 2.15. The backtracking can be seen in the way that the search procedure 'walks round' the perimeter of the state space. The route of the search is not direct, but it does reach the goal eventually. A key question in any specific case is: 'How long is *eventually*?'

29

Activity

Apply the backtracking procedure to find a path from node *k* to node *i* in Figure 2.7. Apply it to find a path from the initial node to the *measles* node in Figure 2.11. Compare the ease with which the procedure copes with the two cases.

A structure for expert systems

The preceding sections have described what expert systems do and how they do it to the extent that it is now possible to perceive a general structure for them.

The state space represents the knowledge that is given to the expert system about the domain in which it is to be applied. If this knowledge is stored as a single unit it can be explored, interrogated or copied. The complete collection of knowledge available to an expert system, or to any other system that deals with knowledge for that matter, is called a *knowledge base*.

The module supporting the process that searches the state space for a path from the initial state to a goal state is kept separate from the knowledge base, although it must obviously have access to the knowledge base. The module that manipulates the knowledge base is called, for reasons that will become clear later, an *inference engine*. The availability of knowledge to help control the search can improve its efficiency. Keeping this knowledge separately ensures that it can be made rapidly available to the search without complicating or confusing the structure of the main knowledge base.

Finally, every program should have a *user interface* that makes it natural and inviting to use by ensuring that requirements are easy to enter and results are well presented. The user interface must interact with the inference engine for most purposes but it should also be able to communicate with the knowledge base so that the knowledge it contains can be examined directly.

These considerations lead to the structure illustrated in Figure 2.16.

Activity

Identify the elements that map on to the knowledge base block and the inference engine block of Figure 2.16 for each of the four example systems described in this chapter.

The principles of operation of expert systems

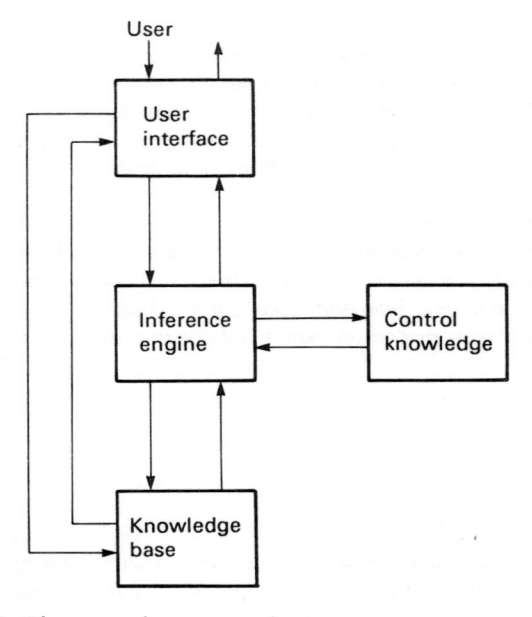

Figure 2.16 *The general structure of an expert system*

Assignment 2

In the role of the programmer at the software house, devise a state transition diagram to model a system. The system is to take its user through a series of stages in order to guide him or her to an appropriate choice of book. (The same structure ought to work for records, videos, college courses and so on.) The first stage is to establish whether the user is interested in fact or fiction. The next stage is to establish whether the user's preference among factual books is for, say, natural history, travel or science. A similar refinement of the fictional choice will be offered. At the next stage, each choice will be further refined with, for example, natural history offering a choice between mammals, reptiles and plants. The reduction of choice will continue in stages until a definite choice of book can be recommended to meet the user's preference.

Advanced Students' Guide to Expert Systems

Recap

- a state transition system is a suitable model for the sorts of activities that have to be carried out by expert systems
- the activities required of an expert system can be modelled in terms of the states the activity can assume and the transitions from one state to another. The transitions are triggered by actions either from outside the system or occurring within it
- an activity is performed by finding a path from an initial state to a state representing the goal of the activity. A path can be found by searching for it
- backtracking is necessary to prevent the search process from failing by getting trapped in a dead-end or caught in a loop
- the requirements placed on expert systems impose a basic structure on them.

Answers to questions

1. IF state = bottom and action = step up THEN state = 1st step
   IF state = 1st step and action = step up THEN state = 2nd step
   and so on.
2. The diagram has five nodes. Action3 would be to give 5p change, while action4 would be to reject the coin.
3. The initial state is 0–0. After the first point of the game, the state will be one of 15–0 and 0–15. After two points, the state will be one of 30–0, 15–15 and 0–30. The diagram can be developed by levels in this way, and eventually a level will be reached that has already occurred.
4. The initial state is (W, W, W). From here the system can fail to one of (F, W, W), (W, F, W) and (W, W, F). After two failures, the state will be one of (F, F, W), (F, W, F) and (W, F, F). There are two transitions from each one-failure state to a two-failure state. Finally, after three failures, the state is (F, F, F).
5. There are 85 different states.
6. If the initial state is (3, 3, w), [3 cannibals and 3 missionaries yet to cross, and the boat on the west bank], the possible successors are (2, 3, e), (1, 3, e), (2, 2, e), (3, 2, e) and (3, 1, e). The last two states are ruled out as unsafe because the cannibals outnumber the missionaries. The first state is inevitably succeeded by the initial state. This leaves only two states to be developed. The process continues as for the problem of the farmer, wolf, goat and cabbage. Take care that the cannibals who have crossed never outnumber the missionaries who have.

3: More on state spaces and search

Objectives

After reading this chapter, you should be able to:
- define the degree of connectivity of a state space
- appreciate the interaction between the degree of connectivity of a space and the ease of searching it
- recognize graph- and tree-structured state spaces
- convert graph-structured spaces to tree-structure spaces
- understand the idea of an implicitly defined state space
- appreciate the concept of *generate and test* as applied to searching an implicitly defined state space
- use the procedures for depth-first, breadth-first and best-first search
- appreciate that the structure of a state space implies a corresponding structure for the dialogue between the user and the system based on that state space model.

The structure of state spaces

Connectivity

A consideration of the possible structures of state spaces in terms of their connectivity gives some insight into how their structure affects the ease with which they may be searched. At one extreme is the structure in which all the states of the space are connected directly to each other. This fully-connected arrangement dictates that a space of n states has $n(n-1)$ arcs. No matter how an initial state and goal state are selected in such a space, they must be connected by a single arc, and the path between them consisting of this one arc can be found by scanning the arcs from the initial state.

Advanced Students' Guide to Expert Systems

The *degree of connectivity* of a space of n states can be defined as the ratio of the number of arcs in the space to that of the fully connected network of n states. This makes the degree of connectivity of a fully connected network *1*, by definition. The space of Figure 2.6 has 13 states and 30 arcs, so that its degree of connectivity is $30/(13 \times 12) = 0.19$. The examples of the previous chapter have shown that there are paths, without loops, between states on opposite sides of the space shown in this figure consisting of 4, 5 and 6 arcs and, in general, there are alternative routes between any initial state and a goal state. The search process, though, cannot find one of them unless it is able to backtrack to get itself out of a dead end.

A structure with a low degree of connectivity is the chain with joined ends, or ring, in which each state is connected to only two neighbours. A space of n states will have $2n$ transitions, making its degree of connectivity $2/(n-1)$. Searching for a path in a space with this structure is trivial, as a path in one direction along the chain, or round the ring, leads from the initial state to every other and so, inevitably, to the goal state.

The main points to be taken from this are the following. In a space in which the states are all connected, there will be a path between any two states. This path will not be difficult to find if the degree of connectivity is very high or very low: spaces with intermediate degrees of connectivity are the hardest to search. But no matter how hard it is to find, the number of arcs in a (non-looping) path from initial state to goal cannot exceed the number of states in the space, because if every state has been visited the goal must have been, too. If a space consists of two or more separate and unconnected parts, it is impossible to find a path from an initial state in one part to a goal state in another.

Question 1

In a space with *n* states, each state is linked by arcs to three others.
   (i) find the degree of connectivity of this space
   (ii) show that the configuration described is not possible if *n* is odd
   (iii) in what circumstances is the degree of connectivity 0.6?

Question 2

A state space has *n* states labelled from *0* to *n-1*. The states are connected as follows: for *i = 0* to *n – 1*, state *i* is connected to state *i + 1* (modulo *n*) and to state *i + 2* (modulo *n*). (With modulo *n* arithmetic, only the numbers from *0* to

More on state spaces and search

n-1 are allowed. Numbers greater than *n-1* must be brought into this range by subtracting *n* as often as necessary. Numbers less than *0* are brought into range by adding *n*.)

(i) how many arcs are there in this space?
(ii) find the degree of connectivity of the space.
(iii) find the length of the shortest path from node *i* to node *j* in this space.

Form

We have already met two significantly different structural forms for state spaces: Figures 2.11 and 2.6 illustrate typical examples of each kind. The structure shown in Figure 2.11 is usually referred to as a *tree*. (It has been drawn on its side compared with, say, an oak tree. To make things worse, in computer science, trees are usually drawn upside down.) The essential point about a tree structure is that it does not contain any loops. The structure illustrated in Figure 2.6, by contrast, contains loops in plenty: we will refer to a structure with loops as a *graph*. As far as searching is concerned, trees are preferable to graphs – as a tree has no loops, there is no need to bother about the search path getting stuck in a loop and, correspondingly, no need to take precautions to prevent it. Also, the potential search paths are to some extent separated already, so that by following the structure of the tree the search process is well-matched to the state space.

Fortunately, a graph can be converted to a tree. In this way, a space with the structure of a graph can be converted to an equivalent tree-structured space. Although, in principle, the tree is easier to search, there will be more states in the equivalent tree structure because some of the states from the graph will appear more than once so that the benefits of conversion are not completely clear cut. One consequence giving a definite benefit from our point of view is that the methods for searching a tree are much simpler than those for a graph.

Figure 3.1 shows a small state space with the structure of a graph, and Figure 3.2 the corresponding tree-structured space. The branches of the tree have been stopped at the point at which the next state to be added would be one that already appears, which is to say, when the corresponding loop from the graph has been 'straightened out'. No branch of the tree contains more than 5 states, which is the number of states in the graph, but the graph of 5 states has given rise to a tree with 12 states.

The procedure for converting a graph to a tree is given below. It makes use of the notion of a pair consisting of a state and a level, which means

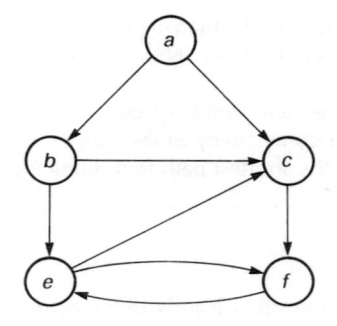

Figure 3.1 A graph

only that a state and a level are associated one with another by bracketing them together thus: (state, level). The procedure is:

- set *LEVEL* to 1
- set *WAITING* to [(initial state, *LEVEL*)]
- set *DONE* to [ ]

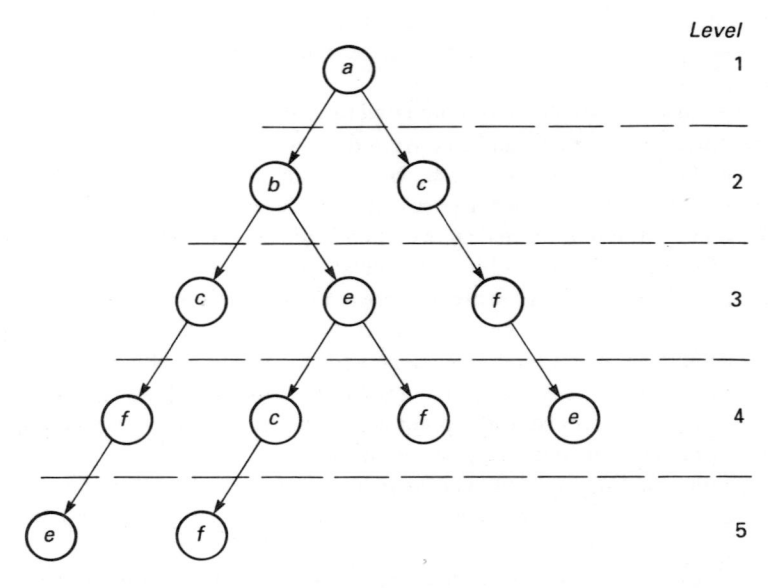

Figure 3.2 *The tree corresponding to Figure 3.1*

More on state spaces and search

- repeat
  - add 1 to *LEVEL*
  - take first pair from *WAITING* and call it (X, Y)
  - if X is the first part of a pair in *DONE*
    then remove pairs from *DONE* until reaching a pair with level one less than the level of the first pair of *WAITING*
    else find the successors of X; form the pairs (X, *LEVEL*); add them to the beginning of *WAITING*, those with states not appearing in *DONE* first and the rest with their states in the same order as in *DONE*;
    add X to the tree at level Y (*DONE* gives the branch leading to it)
  until WAITING is empty

The operation of the procedure can be illustrated by showing the way in which it converts Figure 3.1 to 3.2. From the initial node a, the following sequence of events traces the contents of the lists *WAITING* and *DONE*.

WAITING	*DONE*
Initialise	
[(a, 1)]	[]

Find successors of a. Add a to tree at level 1
[(b, 2), (c, 2)]   [(a, 1)]

Find successors of b. Add b to tree at level 2
[(c, 3), (e, 3), (c, 2)]   [(b, 2), (a, 1)]
[(f, 4), (e, 3), (c, 2)]   [(c, 3), (b, 2), (a, 1)]
[(e, 5), (e, 3), (c, 2)]   [(f, 4), (c, 3), (b, 2), (a, 1)]

The successors of e are f and c. Both appear in *DONE*, and must be added in the same order. (At this point, *DONE* lists the 5 states on the first branch of the tree to be completed)
[(f, 6), (c, 6), (e, 3), (c, 2)]   [(e, 5), (f, 4), (c, 3), (b, 2), (a, 1)]

Now f in the first pair of *WAITING* appears in the second pair of *DONE*. This tries to cause backtracking
[(c, 6), (e, 3), (c, 2)]   [(e, 5), (f, 4), (c, 3), (b, 2), (a, 1)]

c in the first pair of *WAITING* appears in the third pair of *DONE*, causing backtracking to b
[(e, 3), (c, 2)]   [(b, 2), (a, 1)]

e is added to the tree at level 3 on a new branch below b
[(c, 4), (f, 4), (c, 2)]   [(e, 3), (b, 2), (a, 1)]
[(f, 5), (f, 4), (c, 2)]   [(c, 4), (e, 3), (b, 2), (a, 1)]

37

Advanced Students' Guide to Expert Systems

(Another branch is complete. It shares a and b with the first one)
[(e, 6), (f, 4), (c, 2)]   [(f, 5), (c, 4), (e, 3), (b, 2), (a, 1)]
e in the first pair of *WAITING* appears in the third pair of *DONE*. This causes backtracking to e
[(f, 4), (c, 2)]   [(e, 3), (b, 2), (a, 1)]
f is added to the tree at level 3 below starting a third branch
[(e, 5), (c, 2)]   [(f, 4), (e, 3), (b, 2), (a, 1)]
e is in *WAITING* and causes backtracking to a
[(c, 2)]   [(a, 1)]
c is added to the tree at level 2, below a, on a new branch
[(f, 3)]   [(c, 2), (a, 1)]
[(f, 3)]   [(c, 2), (a, 1)]
[(e, 4)]   [(f, 3), (c, 2), (a, 1)]
The successors of e are c and f. Both appear in *WAITING*
[(f, 5), (c, 5)]   [(e, 4), (f, 3), (c, 2), (a, 1)]
[(c, 5)]   [(e, 4), (f, 3), (c, 2), (a, 1)]
[]   [(e, 4), (f, 3), (c, 2), (a, 1)]

The procedure comes to an end with *WAITING* empty and the tree built.

The procedure is easier to carry out than it is to describe. The main reason for presenting it is that its existence allows us to concentrate on the comparatively simple tree-searching methods without any loss of generality. It is worth noting that its general form is much the same as that of the backtracking procedure presented in the previous chapter.

Activity

Use the procedure for converting a graph-structured space to a tree-structured space to convert the graphs of Figures 2.3 and 2.1 to trees.

The implicit description of state spaces

The state spaces we have considered so far have been represented explicitly in that they have been shown in full with all their states and transitions. There are occasions when it may not be desirable to have to

More on state spaces and search

deal with the complete representation of a state space, as when the search for a path is likely to visit only a small part of the space, or when the space is large and requires a correspondingly large amount of storage to hold it. In circumstances like these, it may be desirable to develop the state space as it is needed, by starting from the initial state and repeatedly generating the next states. A description of a state space that consists of an initial state and a mechanism for generating successor states is called an implicit state space description.

This form of description can be illustrated with reference to the 'farmer, wolf, goat and cabbage' problem from the previous chapter. As a brief reminder, the state description chosen for this problem is (F, W, G, C), where F denotes the position of the farmer, W that of the wolf, and so on. The position is denoted by either e (for east) or w (for west). The initial state, as before, is (e, e, e, e) with all four participants on the east bank. This state, and any other, can have up to four successors. They correspond to the farmer rowing across by himself, the farmer rowing across with the wolf, the farmer rowing across with the goat and the farmer rowing across with the cabbage. Of course, some of these activities may not be possible, while others may lead to unsafe situations. After introducing the following definition of 'opposite':

opposite(e) = w

opposite(w) = e,

rules for generating the successor states of (F, W, G, C) can be written as:

1 (opposite(F), W, G, C) is a successor
2 if F = W then (opposite(F), opposite(W), G, C) is a successor
3 if F = G then (opposite(F), W, opposite(G), C) is a successor
4 if F = C then (opposite(F), W, G, opposite(C)) is a successor.

The way these rules can be used may be illustrated with reference to the state (w, e, w, e).

- (e, e, w, e) is a successor. (The farmer can row across)
- F = w and W = e so it is not true that F = W, and rule 2 gives no successor. (The farmer is on the opposite bank to the wolf so he can't row it across)
- F = w and W = w so it is true that F = W, and rule 3 gives the successor (e, e, e, e). (The farmer and the goat are on the same bank so they can row across together)

39

Advanced Students' Guide to Expert Systems

- $F = w$ and $C = e$ so it is not true that $F = C$, and rule 4 gives no successor. (The farmer is on the opposite bank to the cabbage so he can't row it across.)

A search process can make use of an implicit state space description to find a path from an initial state to a goal state by repeatedly generating successor states and testing to see if one of them is the goal state. As long as a goal state is not located, it may be able to choose the most promising of the successor states to continue the path, that is, the state that is 'nearest' in some sense to the goal. If there is no way to assess the promise of the states, one can always be chosen in some arbitrary fashion.

A *generate and search* procedure, very similar to the backtracking procedure of the previous chapter, that generates next states from an implicit description as it searches a state space for a path can be written as:

- initialization
    WAITING is the list containing just the initial state
    DONE is empty
- repeat
    remove the first state from *WAITING*
    generate its successors and put them at the beginning of *WAITING*
    put the state from *WAITING* at the beginning of *DONE*
- until {*WAITING* is empty *or* the goal state is at the beginning of *DONE*}

Question 3

Draw the state transition diagrams for the following implicitly described state spaces. In each case, the states are labelled by numbers:
  (i) state number of initial state = 1; state number of next state = state number of current state + 2
  (ii) state number of initial state = 1. The state number of the next state is obtained by applying the following rules until one succeeds: IF state number for current state is odd THEN state number of next state = state number of current state + 1; IF (state number of current state)/3 is a whole number THEN state number of next state = (state number of current state)/3; IF state number for current state is even THEN state number of next state = state number of current state + 3
  (iii) state number of initial state = 1. The state number of the next state is obtained by applying the following rules until one succeeds: IF state number for current state = 8 THEN state number of next state = 2; IF

More on state spaces and search

state number of current state is odd THEN state number of next state = state number of current state + 3; IF state number for current state is even THEN state number of next state = state number of current state − 1.

Question 4

Draw the state diagram for the implicitly defined space, with an initial state = (1, 1).
There can be up to eight successor states of any state (X, Y). They are:
- (P, Q) where P = X + 1 and Q = Y + 2 as long as $0 < P < 9$ and $0 < Q < 9$
- (P, Q) where P = X − 1 and Q = Y + 2 as long as $0 < P < 9$ and $0 < Q < 9$
- (P, Q) where P = X + 1 and Q = Y − 2 as long as $0 < P < 9$ and $0 < Q < 9$
- (P, Q) where P = X − 1 and Q = Y − 2 as long as $0 < P < 9$ and $0 < Q < 9$
- (P, Q) where P = X + 2 and Q = Y + 1 as long as $0 < P < 9$ and $0 < Q < 9$
- (P, Q) where P = X − 2 and Q = Y + 1 as long as $0 < P < 9$ and $0 < Q < 9$
- (P, Q) where P = X + 2 and Q = Y − 1 as long as $0 < P < 9$ and $0 < Q < 9$
- (P, Q) where P = X − 2 and Q = Y − 1 as long as $0 < P < 9$ and $0 < Q < 9$

Search

The procedure just presented searches a space exhaustively and systematically. The search is done in *depth first* fashion, proceeding first to the end of the left-most branch and then repeatedly backtracking to explore to the end of the next branch, as illustrated in Figure 2.15. This will work well with small spaces, but becomes impractical with large spaces, where it may spend large amounts of time searching a long branch fruitlessly. Fortunately, it is not the only way to search a space.

The *breadth-first* search procedure searches the tree of Figure 2.14 level by level, as shown in Figure 3.3. The procedure differs from that for depth-first search only in that the newly generated successor states are placed at the end of the list *WAITING* rather than at the beginning. The procedure is:

- initialization
    WAITING is the list containing just the initial state
    DONE is empty
- repeat
    remove the first state from *WAITING*
    generate its successors and put them at the end of *WAITING*
    put the state from *WAITING* at the beginning of *DONE*

Advanced Students' Guide to Expert Systems

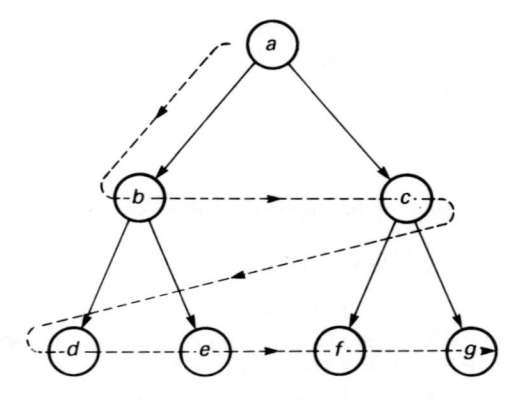

Figure 3.3 Breadth-first search

- until {*WAITING* is empty *or* the goal state is at the beginning of *DONE*}

This procedure also searches a space exhaustively and systematically, and is fine for small spaces where it guarantees to find the optimum solution (that is, to find the shortest path from the initial state to the goal). In a large space, though, it will require a long time to find a goal state that is a long way out on a branch.

Activity

Use the depth-first and breadth-first search procedures to search the space of Figure 3.2. Then compile a list to compare the relative merits of the two search methods.

Neither of these search methods brings any knowledge into play to direct the search, but it is not hard to find a procedure with the same general form that does so. When knowledge of a domain is available in a way that allows states to be assessed for their promise in leading to the goal or for their nearness to the goal, such a procedure may be written as:

- initialization
    WAITING is the list containing just the initial state
    DONE is empty

More on state spaces and search

- repeat
    - assess the states of *WAITING* and remove the most promising
    - generate its successors and put them on *WAITING*
    - put the state from *WAITING* at the beginning of *DONE*
- until {*WAITING* is empty *or* the goal state is at the beginning of *DONE*}

The operation of this procedure can be demonstrated using the abstract example of the tree of Figure 3.4 when the initial state is *a* and the goal is *r*, and the measure of promise of each state is given by:

promise(a) = 0;   promise(b) = 1;   promise(c) = 2;   promise(d) = 3;
promise(e) = 3;
promise(f) = 5;   promise(g) = 4;   promise(m) = 0;   promise(n) = 0;
promise(p) = 0;
promise(q) = 0;   promise(r) = 100;   promise(s) = 0;   promise(t) = 0;
promise(u) = 0;

A trace of the contents of the lists *WAITING* and *DONE* gives:

WAITING	DONE
Initialize	
[a]	[]
Find successors of a	
[b, c]	[a]

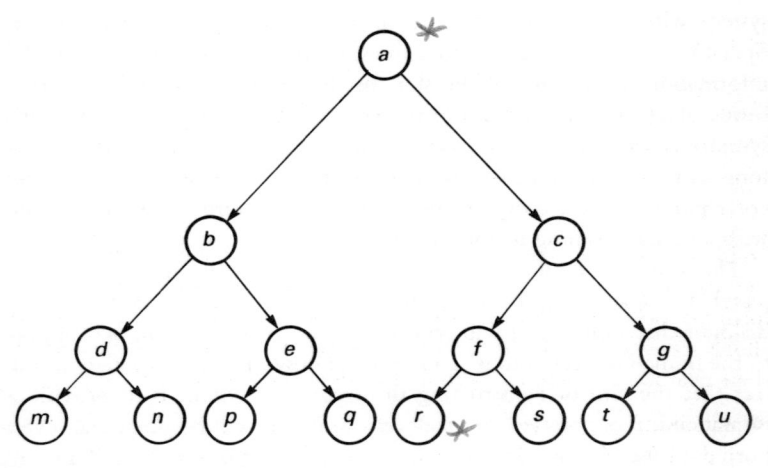

Figure 3.4 *A tree to be searched*

Advanced Students' Guide to Expert Systems

c is the more promising. Its successors are f and g
$[b, f, g]$ $[c, a]$

f is the most promising. Its successors are r and s
$[b, g, r, s]$ $[f, c, a]$

r is the most promising, as it must be, and the goal is reached
$[b, g, r]$ $[r, f, c, a]$

Activity

Explain how knowledge can be incorporated into the 'promise' function by considering specific applications. One such application could be playing noughts and crosses, where the state space develops from an initial state representing the empty grid; the successor states are the grid with a single cross placed on it, and so on. How could 'promise' appear in this case? You could go on to consider, say, draughts and chess.

Some human factors

The idea that a dialogue was embedded in the structure of a state space was introduced in the medical diagnosis example of the previous chapter. It is made clearer, perhaps, by thinking of the states as possessing 'slots', or containers, that can be filled either in advance of the operation of the system with information that has already been acquired, or during its operation with the response to a question designed simply to elicit the information needed to fill the slot. In the diagnosis example, the two forms of operation correspond, respectively, to having all the patient's symptoms prior to trying to make a diagnosis and to obtaining the symptoms as the diagnosis proceeds. The latter is an interactive process, and corresponds to the activity of a doctor trying to determine what is wrong with a patient coming to the surgery.

The structure of the dialogue also depends on the method used to search the space. Depth-first or breadth-first search will give rise to a dialogue that, although it will proceed in a systematic fashion, will appear to the human subjected to it as aimless and unsympathetic. In view of the fact that the aim of constructing the diagnostic system is to provide a human aid, it is pointless to produce a tool that will be unnatural, even boring, to use because this can discourage people from using it. The way to make the system natural to use is to give it the sort of knowledge that an

More on state spaces and search

expert would bring to bear while making a diagnosis so that the search process can be guided in a way that gives rise to the same sort of dialogue as that which would be initiated by the expert. The key is to acquire the knowledge that governs the activity of the human expert at a level that allows it to be transferred to the system to make it behave in a way that is acceptable to the people who use it.

A second issue can be raised in the context of the maintenance technician's advisor, again from the previous chapter, for the system of Figure 2.12. This, or any other advisor, could equally well be used to control a system (in this case to maintain it, perhaps by issuing the appropriate control signals to a robot) as to produce advice. In other words, it could actually *do* something rather than generate advice about what to do. With small systems, it may even be a good idea to allow a bored human to be relieved of a mundane chore and replaced by a machine. With a complex system, matters are rather different. The advisor may be expected to perform well in situations that are well understood, but in areas where its knowledge is incomplete or where the situation has changed since the system was built it cannot always offer reliable advice. Humans adapt to changing circumstances and are used to coping with conflicting knowledge. Knowledge-based systems cannot at present recognize gaps in their knowledge, nor do they 'know what they know'.

The essence of this is that an expert system inevitably has a more limited knowledge of its world than the human expert. To this extent, the human expert is better equipped to deal with complex and rapidly changing situations. An advisory system, of course, can only be of help, but its advice can always be rejected. It could be dangerous to leave such a system in control.

In conclusion, it really ought to be pointed out that the consequences of humans overriding machines can also be horrendous. The accidents at Chernobyl and Three-Mile Island were caused by nothing more than this. The moral is that the people working with machines must also 'know what the machines know', so that when the advice that is offered is in disagreement with their intuition they should not automatically reject it.

Assignment 3

Still in the role of the programmer in the software house, describe the structure of the dialogue implied by the design you produced in Assignment 2. Construct a specific example of the dialogue that would be held with a user with a specific requirement.

Advanced Students' Guide to Expert Systems

Examine the dialogue structures implicit in the designs for the four example systems of the previous chapter. Are any of them more suitable for your application than the one you have designed?

Recap

- the degree of connectivity of a state space is defined as the ratio of the number of arcs in the space to the number in a fully-connected space
- spaces with a high degree of connectivity are easy to search because most states are joined directly to each other, giving trivial search paths. Spaces with a very low degree of connectivity are also easy to search, this time because there are few alternative paths to choose between. Spaces with intermediate degrees of connectivity are the hardest to search
- state spaces can be structured in the form of a graph or a tree. There is a procedure for converting a graph-structured space to an equivalent tree-structured space. Tree-structured spaces are generally simpler to search
- a state space may be described implicitly by giving an initial state and a means of generating the successor states of any state. An implicitly defined space can be searched, starting from the initial state, by repeatedly generating successor states and testing them to see which is the most promising candidate for extending the search path
- procedures are presented for searching a space in depth-first, breadth-first and best-first fashion. Depth-first and breadth-first searches both proceed systematically to visit the states of a space in a fixed order regardless of the application. Best-first search finds solution paths more rapidly than them by using knowledge of the application area to guide the order in which it visits states
- the structure of a state space governs the order in which its states are visited by a search procedure. But each state makes its own contribution to the dialogue, for example, by requesting knowledge that it needs. To this extent, the structure of the space implies an order for the dialogues between the system and its users
- knowledge-based systems can give advice or instigate actions. Their users can accept or reject the advice and, equally, can allow or prevent the actions. But the user who prevents an action, perhaps because it seems inappropriate, must be sure that it really is so. In other words, the user must not only know what the system 'knows' but also be confident of knowing more.

More on state spaces and search

Answers to questions

1 (i) $3/(n-1)$, (ii) The number of arcs in such a space is $3n/2$. If n is odd, then so is $3n$. This requires the space to have half an arc in it! (iii) When $n = 6$, the degree of connectivity is 0.6.
2 (i) There are $2n$ arcs. (ii) The degree of connectivity is $4/(n-1)$. (iii) Find the smaller of i-j (modulo n) and j-i (modulo n). Call it k. If k is even, the shortest path has $k/2$ arcs. If k is odd it has $1 + (k/2)$ arcs.
3 (i) The space is infinite, with state *1* linked to *3*, *3* to *5*, and so on. (ii) The space has four states. State *1* is linked to *2*; *2* to *5*; *5* to *6*; and *6* back to *2*. (iii) The space has seven states. State *1* is linked to *4*; *4* to *3*; *3* to *6*; *6* to *5*; *5* to *8*; *8* to *2*; and *2* back to *1*.
4 The space describes the possible positions for a knight on a chess board after starting from a corner square. The possible positions after one move are (2, 3) and (3, 2).

Pattern Matching

4: Making matters precise

Objectives

After reading this chapter, you should be able to:

- explain what is meant by a function
- determine the type of a function
- write functions for manipulating lists
- express a search procedure as a function
- apply functions that carry out search procedures.

In this chapter a certain amount of mathematics is introduced to allow the ideas and procedures of the previous chapters to be expressed precisely. The concept of a *function* is the main one to be drawn on. A function is essentially a rule for determining the correspondence between the input presented to it and the output delivered by it, as illustrated in Figure 4.1. As a means of converting an input to an output, the function is a mechanism that naturally lends itself to any realm of computing.

The way in which a function is of use may be illustrated by showing how it can carry the implicit description of a tree. Consider the tree of Figure 4.2, where the initial state is a. The successors of a are b and c, and by using a function which can be called *successor*, the rule giving the correspondence between this state and its successors can be written as

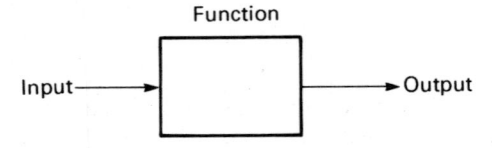

Figure 4.1 *A function as a box with input and output*

Making matters precise

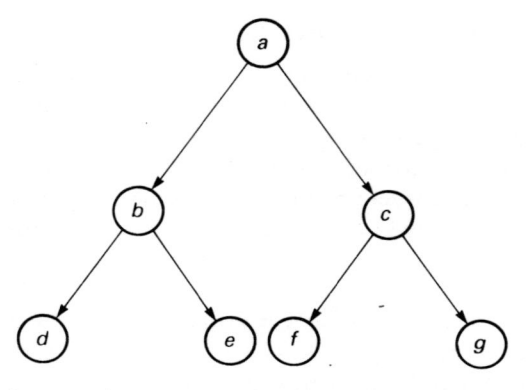

Figure 4.2 A tree to be represented by the function successor

successor(a) = [b, c]. The successor states are written as the members of a list so that no matter how many there are (two, ten or none at all), the correspondence between a state and its successors can be written as a mapping from a state to a list of states. The complete definition of the successor function for Figure 4.2 is:

successor(a) = [b, c]; successor(b) = [d, e]; successor(c) = [f, g]; successor(d) = []; successor(e) = []; successor(f) = []; successor(g) = [].

It is useful to associate with a function the forms of both its input and its output, for in this way any attempt to apply the function to an input of the wrong type can be detected and prevented. For the successor function this information can be written as:

Function: successor; Input: state, Output: list of states.

Question 1

Define the successor function for the tree of Figure 3.2.

Question 2

Give the types of these functions: (i) square – root(x); (ii) integer – part(x); (iii) sum, where, for example, sum([3, 2, 1]) = 3 + 2 + 1 = 6.

Functions for handling lists

A state can be regarded as having zero or more successors or as having a single successor which is a set of (zero or more) states. The output of the 'successor' function uses a list to hold the set of states the members of which are the successors of its input state. In fact, a list can be used to represent a rather stronger structure than a set: because a list of elements is ordered, it can represent an ordered set. The usage of the lists named *WAITING* and *DONE* in the search procedures introduced previously has relied on the fact that a list is an ordered set in requiring the first item to be examined and in adding items at the beginning or the end.

The ordering imposed on a list such as [a, b, c] is the natural one that the item appearing after the opening square bracket (or the left-most item) is the first, with the ordering proceeding from left to right, so that in this case *a* is first, *b* is second and *c* third. The list of zero elements, which is written [], is different from all other lists if only in that because it has no items in it, its items have no order. This list, and only this list, will be referred to as *empty*.

The operations on lists required by the depth-first and breadth-first search procedures are to take the first element from a list and to leave a new list consisting of the old list without its first element. These operations are so commonly required in applications involving lists that special functions are defined to carry them out. The function 'head' is applied to a non-empty list and delivers the first item of that list. The function 'tail' is also applied to a non-empty list and delivers the list with its first item removed. The use of these functions is illustrated by:

- head([a, b, c]) = a
- tail([a, b, c]) = [b, c].

A third function, for adding an item to the beginning of a list, is also of value, not least because it is intimately related to the head and tail functions. The operation of this function, named add, is illustrated by:

- add(f, [a, b, c]) = [f, a, b, c].

A little thought will show that for any list L:

- add(head(L), tail(L)) = L.

The types of these functions are:

> *Function: head; Input: non-empty list of states, Output: state.*
> *Function: tail; Input: non-empty list of states, Output: list of states.*
> *Function: add; Input: state and list of states, Output: list of states.*

Making matters precise

By using these three functions as basic building blocks, it is possible to build other functions for examining lists. A function for counting the number of items in a list, L, for example, can be defined by:

length(L) = if L = [] then 0 else 1 + length((tail(L))

When expressed in English, this definition says that the number of items in a list is zero if the list is empty but otherwise is one (for the first item in the list) plus the number of items in the rest of the list. The way the function works can be illustrated by tracing its operation as it evaluates length([a, b, c]):

length([a, b, c]) = 1 + length(tail([a, b, c]))
    because [a, b, c] is not empty
= 1 + length([b, c])
= 1 + 1 + length(tail([b, c]))
    because [b, c] is not empty
= 1 + 1 + length([c]))
= 1 + 1 + 1 + length(tail([c]))
    because [c] is not empty
= 1 + 1 + 1 + length([])
= 1 + 1 + 1 + 0
    because [] is empty
= 3.

The function 'member(x, L)' which takes the value 'true' if the item x is a member of the list of items L, and takes the value 'false' otherwise is defined by:

member(x, L) = if L = [] then false else
    if head(L) = x then true
    else member(x, tail(L))

The operation of this function can be illustrated by tracing the evaluation of member(b, [a, b, c]).

member(b, [a, b, c]) = member(b, tail([a, b, c]))
    because [a, b, c] is not empty and head([a, b, c]) is not b
= member(b, [b, c])
= true
    because [b, c] is not empty but head([b, c]) is b.

Question 3

Write a function, sum, which when given a list of numbers will deliver the sum of the numbers in the list. Trace the operation of the function in evaluating sum([3, 2, 1]).

Question 4

(i) write a function, delete, which when given an element and a list of elements of the same type will give the list with the element deleted from it. For example, delete(b, [a, b, c]) = [a, c]
(ii) write a function, larger, which when given two lists of numbers having the same length will deliver a single list in which each number is the larger of the two numbers in the corresponding positions of each input list. For example, larger([2, 2, 2, 2], [1, 3, 1, 3]) = [2, 3, 2, 3].

Functions for searching

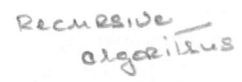

Recursive algorithms

With the capability to describe a state space implicitly, and the basic tools for manipulating lists it is now possible to define functions for the depth-first and breadth-first search of tree-structured state spaces.

An examination of the descriptions of the search procedures shows that the only activity for which a function has yet to be defined is appending one list to another. A function for appending two lists such that, for example, append([a, b], [c, d]) = [a, b, c, d] can be defined as follows:

append(X, Y) = if X = [] then Y else add(head(X), append(tail(X), Y))

This states that appending the lists X and Y gives Y if X is empty but that otherwise the lists can be appended by adding the first item of X to the list obtained by appending the tail of X to Y. A trace of the operation of append([a, b], [c, d]) shows how the function works:

append([a, b], [c, d]) = add(head([a, b]), append(tail([a, b]), [c, d]))
    because [a, b] is not empty
= add(a, append([b], [c, d]))
= add(a, add(head([b]), append(tail([b]), [c, d])))
    because [b] is not empty
= add(a, add(b, append([], [c, d])))

Making matters precise

$$= \text{add}(a, \text{add}(b, [c, d]))$$
    because [] is empty
$$= \text{add}(a, [b, c, d])$$
$$= [a, b, c, d].$$

The type of the append function is:

Function: append; Input: two lists of states, Output: list of states.

This completes all the preliminaries, and a function for depth-first search can be defined. It uses the print function, which prints its input, and is:

dfsearch(goal, waiting, done) =
    if waiting = [] then print('fail') else
    if head(waiting) = goal then print('success') else
    dfsearch(goal, append(successors(head(waiting)), tail(waiting)),
    add(head(waiting), done))

The tree in Figure 4.2 could be searched for the goal *f* by using the successor function defined earlier in the chapter in dfsearch(*f*, [*a*], []). The type of this search function is:

Function: dfsearch; Input: a state and two lists of states, Output: prints 'true' or 'false'.

The function for breadth-first search differs from that for depth-first only in that the two lists are given to append in reverse order. It is:

bfsearch(goal, waiting, done) =
    if waiting = [] then print('fail') else
    if head(waiting) = goal then print('success') else
    bfsearch(goal, append(tail(waiting), successors(head(waiting))),
    add(head(waiting), done))

Its type is the same as that of dfsearch.

Best-first search

To be able to carry out a search by always taking the most promising state from the list of states waiting to be examined, a means of assessing the states is needed. Naturally, this can be done with a function. The rating function, for example, can be used to assign a numerical rating to each state: higher values are supposed to indicate more promising states. The states of Figure 4.2 can be assigned ratings with the following definition:

rating(*a*) = 1; rating(*b*) = 3; rating(*c*) = 2; rating(*d*) = 0; rating(*e*) = 0; rating(*g*) = 0

53

Advanced Students' Guide to Expert Systems

A function to find the better (or more promising) of two states is:

better(a, b) = if rating(a) > rating(b) then a else b.

Before proceeding to write a function for best-first search, two other functions are needed: one to find the best (most promising) item in a list, and another to remove that item from the list as it will not in general be the first one. The best state in a list, L, can be found with:

best(L) = if length(L) = 1 then head(L) else better(head(L), best(tail(L)))

The operation of this function is illustrated by the following trace.

best([a, b, c]) = better(head([a, b, c]), best(tail([a, b, c])))
    because length([a, b, c]) = 3
= better(a, best([b, c]))
= better(a, better(head([b, c]), best(tail([b, c]))))
    because length([b, c]) = 2
= better(a, better(b, best([c])))
= better(a, better(b, c))
    because length([c]) = 1
= better(a, b)
    because rating(b) > rating(c)
= b
    because rating(b) > rating(a)

An item, x, can be removed from a list, L, by the function:

remove(x, L) = if L = [] then [] else
    if head(L) = x then tail(L) else
    add(head(L), remove(x, tail(L))).

With the aid of these ancillary functions, the function for best-first search is defined by:

best-first(goal, waiting, done) =
    if waiting = [] then print('fail') else
    if best(waiting) = goal then print('success') else
    best-first(goal, append(successors(best(waiting)),
    remove(best(waiting), waiting)), add(best(waiting), done))

This function can be used to search the tree of Figure 4.2 for the goal f in the form best-first(f, [a], []).

Making matters precise

Activity

Trace the operation of the functions dfsearch, bfsearch and best-first in searching the tree of Figure 3.2. Before tracing best-first, define a function rating over the states of the space.

Assignment 4

Again in the role of the programmer in the software house, return to your system design of Assignment 2. First, write a function to represent the state transition diagram. Then write a function, analogous to the search functions of this chapter, which when applied will carry out the progressive narrowing-and-selection operation by which the system homes in on a suitable choice of book for its user. Trace an application of the second function to see if it works properly.

As well as this, go to your library and find a book on functional programming. Use this book to find out how programming in terms of functions is done in practice so that you can justify your approach to writing the system to your project supervisor and also recommend a programming language.

Recap

- a function is essentially a way of determining the outputs corresponding to the inputs that it may be given. A function is used by applying it to its input so that it may deliver the corresponding output
- the type of a function is specified by giving the types of its input and output. Taking care to note the type of a function can prevent its misuse
- there are standard functions for handling lists. One accepts a list and delivers the head of the list; the second accepts a list and delivers the tail of the list; and the third accepts an element and a list and delivers a list with the element added to it as its head. In this chapter, these functions have been called head, tail and add.
- a function can be used to give an implicit description of a state space
- with the aid of the standard functions for elementary list manipulation, functions can be written to carry out breadth-first, depth-first and best-first search of a state space
- the function is an entirely suitable formalism for the precise description of state spaces and for the methods available for searching them.

Advanced Students' Guide to Expert Systems

Answers to questions

1. successor(a) = [b, c]; successor(b) = [c, e]; successor(c) = [f]; successor(e) = [c, f]; successor(f) = [e].
2. (i) Function: square – root; Input: real number, Output: real number
   (ii) Function: integer – part; Input: real number, Output: whole number
   (iii) Function: sum; Input: list of numbers, Output: number.
3. sum(L) = if L = [] then 0 else head(L) + sum(tail(L)).
4. (i) see the function 'remove' later in the chapter.
   (ii) larger(List1, List2) =
       if (List1 = [] and List2 = []) then [] else
           if head(List1) > head(List2) then
               add(head(List1), larger(tail(List1), tail(List2))) else
               add(head(List2), larger(tail(List1), tail(List2))).

5: Knowledge and ways of obtaining it

Objectives

After reading this chapter, you should be able to:

- distinguish between knowledge elicitation and knowledge acquisition or, at least, between the concepts given those names in this book
- appreciate the need to represent elicited knowledge in some readily comprehensible form
- understand various methods for eliciting knowledge from experts
- use at least one of these elicitation methods
- choose between these elicitation methods for a specific elicitation task
- understand the methods presented for the automatic elicitation of knowledge
- use the methods presented for the automatic elicitation of knowledge.

Scenario

The hospital's Head of Research has summoned one of his senior scientists.

'We've decided to try and set up an expert system in the hospital to diagnose pulmonary infections.'

'That sounds interesting. What do you want me to do?'

'I need some advice, really. We've decided to get an expert system shell and to give it the expertise about diagnosing the illnesses ourselves.'

'Yes?'

'Well, Dr Newman is an expert on pulmonary illnesses, so we've got the expert. But how on earth do we get at his expertise so that we can put it in the shell?'

'Ah. As it happens, I know this woman who calls herself a knowledge elicitor ...'

Knowledge is basic to the operation of expert systems. The main concerns in the partnership between knowledge and expert systems are the following:

> How does one get the knowledge for an expert system?
> How does one 'fix' it in terms of some suitable representation?
> How does the expert system make use of it?

These matters are essentially separate, and each has its own terminology. The word *elicitation* will be used here to refer to the process of getting (or extracting, or capturing) knowledge, whether from an expert or from an automatic learning system. The result of elicitation is knowledge expressed in a way that is comprehensible to people. The 'fixing' of knowledge by representing it in a way that renders it suitable for the computer will be called knowledge *acquisition*. The point here is that the knowledge has been acquired in such a way that the computer can store it and make use of it. Different terms are used for the process by which the computer makes use of the knowledge and, indeed, expert systems do make use of it in different ways, but these ways all share the common approach of connecting items of knowledge. The term *inference* is taken to indicate this general use of knowledge, although without denying it its specific technical meaning in the study of logic.

People learn in more than one way: they learn, for instance, by being told, by example and from experience. Expert systems can, in principle at least, get their knowledge in the same ways, although learning from experience is rather at the edge of the current state of the technology. They can, though, learn by 'being told', which raises the question of where the knowledge comes from. They can also learn from examples, and the question here is: 'How?'. This chapter attempts to answer some of these questions.

One general point that cannot be stressed too strongly is that one of the aims of knowledge elicitation, whether from an expert or from a learning machine, is to capture knowledge in a form that makes it accessible to people. It is hard to see that experts from whom knowledge has been elicited can confirm that the elicited knowledge really represents their expertise unless it can be presented to them in a form that they can understand. Also, if an expert system is to explain, say, the reasoning behind advice it has offered, it must be able to present, in a form comprehensible to the person receiving the advice, the knowledge that led it to produce that advice.

Knowledge and ways of obtaining it

Eliciting knowledge from an expert

Theories from psychology suggest that we all carry our own model of the world in our minds. The model allows us to classify items and events, to develop our own theories about the world, and to anticipate events in it so that we can plan our actions accordingly. In these terms, an expert is someone with a highly developed model of a particular domain which enables him or her to explain and generally deal with that domain better than most other people. The difference between the models of a non-expert and an expert manifests itself in their different reactions to a situation. The non-technical car driver's response to an unusual noise from his car's engine, for example, might be: 'My car is making a funny noise', while the experienced mechanic might say: 'It sounds as if the timing needs adjusting.' Again, when a novice computer programmer reports that: 'My program doesn't decide properly between theses cases', a more experienced programmer might say that: 'The conditional statements in the program are not properly nested.'

The difficulty with some experts is that their knowledge is held privately. When the knowledge is of mathematics or quantum physics, it will also be recorded in books and papers, because the expert mathematicians and physicists have recorded their knowledge. With access to the printed material, newcomers to these subjects have the potential to become the experts of the future. When the knowledge is of matters such as troubleshooting, diagnosis and what we might call 'black arts', the knowledge tends to be private to the experts, with consequences that include the complete loss of the knowledge when an expert dies and the loss of access to knowledge when an expert leaves a company. Thus, there are reasons for eliciting knowledge from an expert other than to make it available to an expert system.

The general aim of knowledge elicitation is to formalize the knowledge of the expert in a style in which it can be communicated both to the expert and to the knowledge engineer who will convert it to a form suitable for inclusion in an expert system.

The knowledge elicitor can employ any of a variety of techniques to get at the expert's privately held knowledge. They can be classified into groups that include interviewing, the use of examples, problem solving and methods based on theories from psychology. These four families of methods are described in turn in the rest of this section. Some of the specific methods are suitable for the automatic elicitation of knowledge (although they can be used without being automated) and they are collected in the next section.

59

Interviewing

A knowledge elicitor approaches the task of interviewing an expert with no preconceived ideas about the knowledge domain and in a spirit of genuine enquiry. The elicitor cannot possibly be familiar with the domains of expertise of all the experts he may encounter over a period of time, and it can be argued that it is an advantage to come to a domain with no knowledge at all of it, for then there can be no preconceptions. These considerations also show that the elicitor must be able to learn quickly in a new domain, and must know how to learn.

The expert may need to be put at ease and encouraged to speak freely, but then the elicitor must get him to talk about his expertise so that the knowledge essential to that expertise may be revealed. The elicitor is trying to identify the basic elements to which the expertise applies, the relationships between them and, ultimately, the structure on which the expert's 'cloth of knowledge' is hung. In essence, the elicitor brings what might be called a *heightened common sense* to the interview, scattering questions like: 'What do you mean by ...?', 'How do you know that?' and 'How did you reach that conclusion?' throughout the interview. Besides enquiring, the elicitor is educating himself, albeit in a rather more active and directed way than that suffered by most students undergoing formal education. Because of his active role, the elicitor must be careful not to impose anything of himself during the interview either to interfere with the expert's knowledge or with his way of exposing it. The sole aim is to direct the interview towards the ultimate goal of elicitation.

There are aids that can be employed, ranging from the use of a questionnaire to standard interviewing techniques such as free association, but an elicitor with a firm grip on his own approach to interviewing may be able to proceed without them. Even so, some supplementary reading, perhaps from textbooks or manuals, will almost certainly be needed at some stage. The elicitor may also find it helpful to observe the expert in the act of doing his job, and also to interview him while doing his job, rather than just doing 'cold' interviews.

Of course, elicitation is not a one-way process. When the elicitor has followed his observe-note-react cycle to the point that he feels he has elicited at least some worthwhile aspect of the expert's knowledge, he changes roles with the expert to explain the knowledge that he has elicited. The point of the exercise is to let the expert judge whether his knowledge has been captured properly. The elicitor's attitude is now one of enquiring whether the elicited model is correct: the expert can confirm

Knowledge and ways of obtaining it

it or, if it is not correct, can locate the points in error. In this way, the elicitor, having learnt from the expert, teaches back what he has learnt to examine its accuracy. The judgement of the expert is absolute at this stage. The dialogue continues for as long as is necessary to gain agreement.

An example that shows rather startlingly that knowledge elicitation can achieve results that enlighten even the expert from whom the knowledge is elicited concerns an operator whose job was to pour ingredients into a smelting furnace at a time he felt was right to ensure their correct combination. He carried out this task with unvarying success but, when asked, could not explain how. By dint of careful observation and enquiry, it was found that he started to pour when the flame of the furnace was a particular colour. It was found later that this colour corresponded exactly to the optimum temperature for the occurrence of the chemical processes involved in the smelting.

Examples

An elicitor can focus his interaction with an expert with the aid of examples. At one extreme, the expert can be asked to give examples that typify the activities he carries out in the course of displaying his expertise, while at the other the elicitor may devise a standard structured framework and then ask the expert to give a set of examples of his activities to fit it. Examples of the first kind may be quite easy to obtain, but they are, in general, difficult to analyse. They will contain some of the concepts of the domain, and some of the relations between them, but it is difficult to ensure that all the concepts and relations of the domain are represented. It should, though, be possible to tease out the knowledge that is present to get the same kind of result as from interviewing. Standard examples may not always be sufficiently flexible to catch the domain knowledge, but they are easy to analyse. In fact, they can be analysed automatically, and a method for this is described later. In summary, then:

1 It is almost certainly too difficult to tease complete domain knowledge out of completely unstructured examples
2 Structured examples may be able to capture some limited aspect of the domain knowledge, but are usually too limited to deal with an entire domain.

The remedy may be to use one of the following:

- a combination of the two approaches

Advanced Students' Guide to Expert Systems

- some kind of loose structuring for the examples
- several sets of structured examples, with one set for different aspects of the domain.

When eliciting by means of examples it should always be remembered that the quality of the elicited knowledge depends on how good the examples are, that is to say, on how well they represent the domain. The expert should be asked to assess the representativeness of each set of examples that he generates, but this is not easy. It is one thing to be sure that every example illustrates a domain activity, but quite another to be sure that each domain activity is represented by an example.

Knowledge elicitation by means of examples is a valuable technique in itself, but it can also be used to complement other methods. It assumes even more value in supporting a means for the automatic elicitation of knowledge. Taking this a step further, adding an automatic learning capability at the front-end of an expert system can give the system the ability to generate its own knowledge once it has been supplied with a set of examples.

Problem solving   *Observation, protocol analysis*

The activity of some experts overtly consists of solving problems, while that of others can be regarded as such even though it may not be conventionally thought of in this way. An expert trouble-shooter, for instance, is certainly a problem-solver. A doctor making a diagnosis is also solving a problem, that of what is wrong with his patient (at least, he is if he does it successfully) although it is not usual to talk about doctors' work in this way.

After explaining the problem-solving point of view to an expert, if that is necessary, an elicitor can ask the expert to describe aloud exactly what he is doing either in the course of solving a problem or to explain his actions afterwards. Neither approach is entirely satisfactory because it can be distracting for the expert to talk while he is working, especially at the points where his actions are the most intuitive so that he performs them 'without thinking'. The very points where the expert's thinking about what he is doing may prove disruptive are precisely those that are most critical to the elicitor. When talking afterwards, the expert tends to gloss over the very same critical points. One way of escaping from this impasse is for the elicitor to film the expert in action and to discuss the filmed activity. The discussion can then take place at one and the same time during the (filmed) action and after the (actual) event.

Knowledge and ways of obtaining it

Activity

Try to express your own expertise in a problem-solving activity by explaining how you go about solving an equation in one variable or determining a definite integral.

Psychological techniques

One of the more widely used techniques based on a psychological theory is that of the *repertory grid*. It has its basis in personal construct psychology which, as outlined briefly at the beginning of this chapter, suggests that we are all 'scientists' with our personal models of the world, and that we use our models as a basis from which to develop our own theories about the world. The repertory grid is a way of attempting to capture this model. Because everyone has a unique model that is personal to them, they will, in general, also fill in a repertory grid in a unique way. This can be turned to advantage in the case of an expert because it is precisely his personal knowledge that makes him an expert, and this knowledge can be captured in his repertory grid.

The skeleton of a repertory grid is a table of *elements* and *constructs*. An element is an example or instance of an entity in the domain. A construct is a characteristic that is possessed to some degree by all the elements. Thus, if the entities of a domain were animals, the constructs could include heavy–light, large–small and brightly coloured–dull. Note that a construct covers a range between two extremes: a particular animal may be heavy, light or anything in between. The skeleton for a simple repertory grid could take the form shown in Figure 5.1. The grid can be filled in by using the values 10 and 1 to denote that an element possesses a construct to the degree corresponding to the respective extremes on the left and right of the skeleton. That is, a heavy animal is rated at 10 for the heavy–light construct, and a light one at 1. The value is scaled correspondingly when an element possesses the characteristic of the construct to some intermediate degree. The grid of Figure 5.1 could be filled in as shown in Figure 5.2.

The skeleton of a grid will usually be devised by an elicitor as a means of representing his view of the structure of the domain knowledge. By filling in the grid, an expert (or anyone else) records his knowledge of the domain: in this way, the expert's knowledge is being elicited when he fills in the grid.

Advanced Students' Guide to Expert Systems

	Elements			
	Elephant	Tiger	Mouse	
Constructs { Large Bright Heavy				Small Dull } Constructs Light

10 ——————————————— 1

5.1 *Skeleton for a repertory grid*

	Elements			
	Elephant	Tiger	Mouse	
Large	10	5	1	Small
Bright	1	9	2	Dull
Heavy	10	5	1	Light

5.2 *Filled in repertory grid*

Different people will fill in a grid differently, so that a repertory grid provides a way of comparing peoples' knowledge of a domain. Grids can be analysed and refined, by removing redundancy and drawing distinctions, to express the knowledge they represent in an alternative, perhaps more compact, form. As there are automatic methods for refining and analysing grids, they will be covered in the next section.

Activity

Consider the task of eliciting the expertise of an expert lecturer. Select a lecturer whom you judge to be expert, and decide which of the techniques of this section you would choose to elicit his or her expertise. Explain the reasons for your choice. Would you consider employing more than one technique? If you decided to tackle a second expert, would you use the same means of elicitation?

Automatic means of elicitation

The methods of eliciting knowledge described in this section are sufficiently well defined to be carried out automatically. They can, of course

Knowledge and ways of obtaining it

be carried out by people as well as by machines. The reason for gathering the methods together here is that the prospect of automatic knowledge elicitation opens up realms beyond those that can be reached using the labour-intensive methods of a human elicitor.

Learning from examples   *induction*

The requirements for extracting knowledge from examples are:

1. A set of examples to work on
2. A set of attributes or characteristics to describe each example. When, for instance, the examples are of medical diagnosis, the attributes of each diagnosis could be the patient's symptoms: the characteristics of each member of a set of objects could be chosen to be its size, shape and colour
3. A set of classes to represent the classification of each example in the set. A patient would be classified as having a particular disease; an object could be classified as being large and red
4. A method for extracting the knowledge, which will depend on both the form of the examples and the form required for the elicited knowledge.

To illustrate the methods of this section, the examples are provided by the capital letters of the alphabet. Their attributes have been chosen as the number of straight lines in a letter, the number of curves, and the number of joins, either of two lines or of a line and a curve. Thus, for a the letter P, the attributes take the values:

- number of lines = 1
- number of curves = 1
- number of joins = 1.

From examples to rules

The knowledge contained in a set of examples can be converted to knowledge expressed in the form of rules by organizing the attribute values as a tree. The process is most easily explained by considering Table 5.1, which shows four examples which have been classified into two sets.

The tabulated attribute values can be organized into a tree structure, as shown in Figure 5.3, by choosing the attribute *number of joins* for the root of the tree, the attribute *number of curves* for the next level, and the

Advanced Students' Guide to Expert Systems

Table 5.1 Four examples, classified into two sets

Example	Attributes		Class
	Number of curves	Number of joins	
1	0	2	A
2	1	2	B
3	0	1	A
4	1	1	B

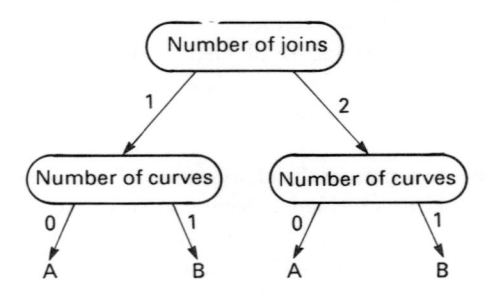

Figure 5.3 Classification: first attempt

appropriate classification for the leaf of the tree at the end of each branch. The tree is an alternative way of representing the table, but the knowledge it contains can be read from it in the form of rules. The left-most branch, for example, can be read as:

IF number of joins = 1 AND number of curves = 0 THEN classification is A

The tree gives four rules, with one for each example, so that although the form of the knowledge has been changed, it has not been refined at all. The essence of the knowledge has not been distilled.

A tree could have been obtained by choosing the attributes in a different order: it is shown in Figure 5.4. This tree is organized in a way that has successfully classified the examples, as the left-hand branch from the root leads to the examples in class A and the right-hand one to those in class B. Furthermore, the second decision is unnecessary to the classification process, as illustrated in Figure 5.5 where each branch leads to examples of only one class. The classification rules can be read from Figure 5.4 as:

Knowledge and ways of obtaining it

```
              ┌─────────────────┐
              │ Number of curves│
              └─────────────────┘
              0 /           \ 1
     ┌────────────────┐  ┌────────────────┐
     │ Number of joins│  │ Number of joins│
     └────────────────┘  └────────────────┘
        1 /    \ 2          1 /    \ 2
          A      A             B      B
```

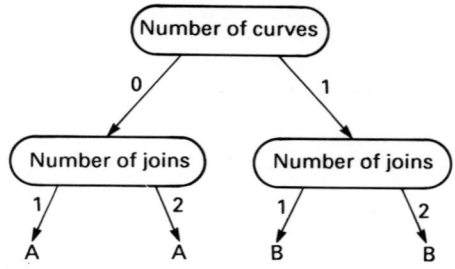

Figure 5.4 *Classification: second attempt*

```
         ┌──────────┐
         │  Number  │
         │ of curves│
         └──────────┘
         0 /      \ 1
           A        B
```

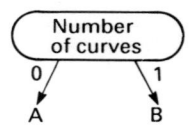

Figure 5.5 *Reduction of classification tree of Figure 5.4*

IF number of curves = 0 THEN class is A
IF number of curves = 1 THEN class is B

This time, the essential knowledge has been elicited to be expressed in the form of rules.

The method, then, is to organize the attribute values as a tree, finding the best order in which to take the attributes. The problem remains of how to find the best order. One approach is to try all possible orderings, and this may be feasible when the number of attributes is small although it is not for a large number. (Given n attributes, there are factorial (n) orderings, that is:

$n(n-1)(n-2) \ldots \times 2 \times 1$ orderings. Factorial(10), for instance, is greater than 3.5 million.)

The key to finding the best ordering for the attributes is to start with the attribute that is most informative in the sense that, by itself, it goes the furthest towards making the classification. This attribute can be found by direct comparison of all the attributes. With the first attribute selected, the next one can be found in exactly the same way, and the process can be repeated until all the attributes have been ordered. Table 5.2 should help to clarify this.

The tree for Table 5.2 is shown in Figure 5.6: the attributes have been ordered in no particular way. Figure 5.7 shows the results of assessing each attribute as a candidate for starting the tree, with these results:

Advanced Students' Guide to Expert Systems

Table 5.2 Eight examples classified into two sets

Example	Number of lines	Number of curves	Number of joins	Class
	Attributes			
1	1	1	0	B
2	1	1	1	A
3	0	1	0	B
4	1	1	1	A
5	3	0	1	B
6	1	0	0	A
7	2	0	1	B
8	2	0	0	A

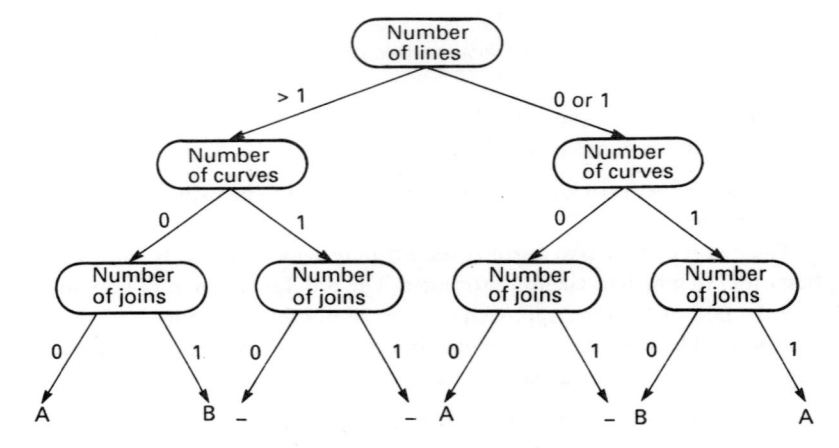

Figure 5.6 An attempt at classification

a *number of lines* – values greater than 1 give one example in class A and two in class B, that is, one correct classification and two that are wrong. A value of 0 or 1 gives three examples in class A and two in class B, that is two right and three wrong. In all, there are five wrong classifications

b *number of curves* – a value of 0 gives two examples in class A and two in class B, that is two right and two wrong. A value of 1 gives the same result. In all, there are four wrong classifications

c *number of joins* – this gives the same result as does the number of curves.

Knowledge and ways of obtaining it

```
        (Number of lines)
        >1/        \0 or 1
       1 in A      3 in A
       2 in B      2 in B
(a)
```

```
        (Number
         of curves)
        0/        \1
       2 in A     2 in A
       2 in B     2 in B
(b)
```

```
        (Number of joins)
        0/        \1
       2 in A     2 in A
       2 in B     2 in B
(c)
```

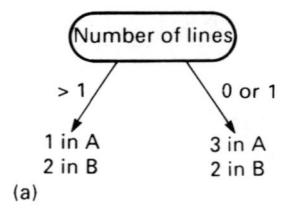

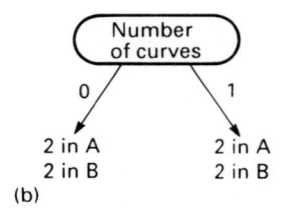

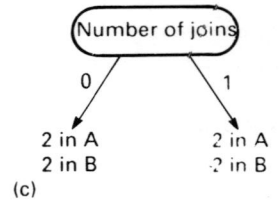

Figure 5.7 *Assessing the attributes as a basis for ordering them*

From this, it can be seen that the *number of curves* and the *number of joins* are equally good, and that both are better than the *number of lines*. This suggests that either the *number of curves* or the *number of joins* should be taken first, and that, whichever is chosen, the other should be second. The resulting tree is shown in Figure 5.8. The fact that each of its branches leads to a correct classification shows that the essential knowledge held in the examples can be expressed in terms of the two attributes used for the tree. The classification rules are:

IF number of joins = 0 AND number of curves = 0 THEN class is A
IF number of joins = 0 AND number of curves = 1 THEN class is B
IF number of joins = 1 AND number of curves = 0 THEN class is B
IF number of joins = 1 AND number of curves = 1 THEN class is A

Advanced Students' Guide to Expert Systems

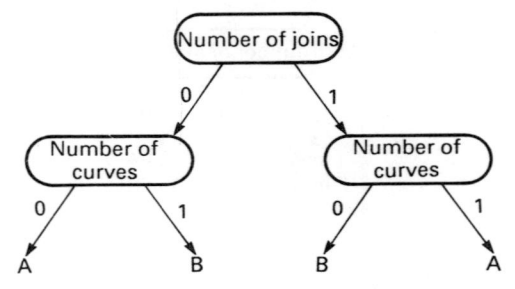

Figure 5.8 *Classification with the attributes in preferred order*

They can be expressed more compactly as the two rules:

IF (number of joins = 0 AND number of curves = 0) OR (number of joins = 1 AND number of curves = 1) THEN class is A

IF (number of joins = 0 AND number of curves = 1) OR (number of joins = 1 AND number of curves = 0) THEN class is B

The examples of this section illustrate the principle of a method for obtaining rules from a set of examples. A method known as *ID3* uses the same principles and adds to them a numerical criterion, based on ideas from information theory, to determine precisely the best choice of attribute at each stage of the tree.

Question 1

Extract the essential knowledge from Table 5.3 in the form of rules.

Table 5.3 *Knowledge for Question 1*

Example	Size	Attributes Colour	Texture	Class
1	L	Red	Rough	Unappealing
2	M	Blue	Rough	Appealing
3	L	Red	Rough	Unappealing
4	L	Red	Smooth	Appealing
5	M	Red	Smooth	Appealing
6	M	Red	Rough	Unappealing
7	L	Blue	Smooth	Appealing
8	L	Blue	Rough	Appealing

Knowledge and ways of obtaining it

Training by examples

This method described here is for training a system to recognize any member of a set, and only members of that set, with the aid of a carefully selected set of examples. The training examples are introduced to the system in succession, and each is presented as either a representative of the set to be recognized (or, what is the same thing, the concept to be learnt) or as a 'near miss'. The property of a near miss is that it is almost, but not quite, an instance of the concept: ideally, it should fail to be an instance in one simple and clear respect.

An expert may be needed to train the system, because the selection of the examples is vitally important, both in the choice of representative instances and in the judgement of what constitutes a near miss. The trainer may also need a good understanding of how the system itself works to be able to present the examples in the most effective order.

The system, which is to be trained to recognize capital letters, is assumed to have the following properties:

- it can recognize the basic features from which letters are composed, that is, straight lines and curves
- it can recognize the relative positions of the features in terms of left, centre, right, top and bottom
- it can recognize basic relations between features in terms of whether a feature either 'ends on' or 'adjoins' (touches with any point other than its end) another
- it can compare two descriptions and detect the difference between them.

Thus, the system can recognize, for example, that a capital L consists of two lines each of which ends on the other. Similarly, it can recognize that a capital Q consists of a line and a curve. The line adjoins the curve, and the curve adjoins the line.

Now, let us turn to the task of training this system to recognize a capital H. It could first be shown an H (in a commonly used fount, such as this one) as an example, from which it could build the description shown in Figure 5.9. This description may seem quite adequate, but if the system is to recognize this letter when presented with it in a number of different founts and styles, and even when hand-written, it may need a more robust description. If it is next shown a capital A as a near miss, the system will generate the description shown in Figure 5.10, and detect that the difference between this and its existing description of H is that the left-hand and

Advanced Students' Guide to Expert Systems

right-hand lines touch. This difference is the reason for the near miss, and so must not be possessed by the description of the H, which can be amended as shown in Figure 5.11 by forbidding the cause of the difference. Showing a broken H, in which the horizontal line does not meet the two verticals, to the system as a second near miss causes a different kind of change to the description of H. The description of the broken H is shown in Figure 5.12: it differs by not possessing the *ends on* and *adjoins* relations. As this absence is the cause of the near miss, the system deduces that the absence of these relations is not allowed, and so requires them, as shown in Figure 5.13.

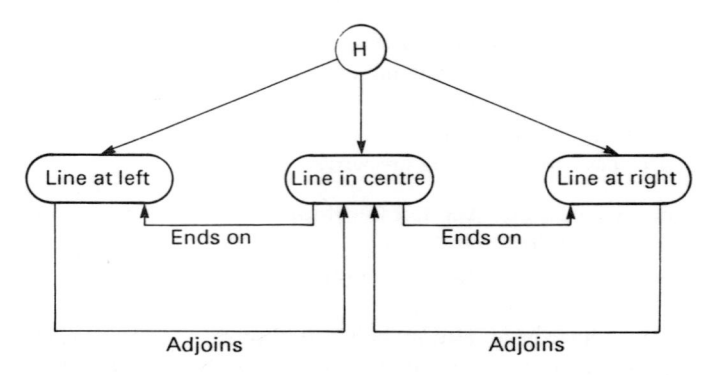

Figure 5.9 *Initial description of an H*

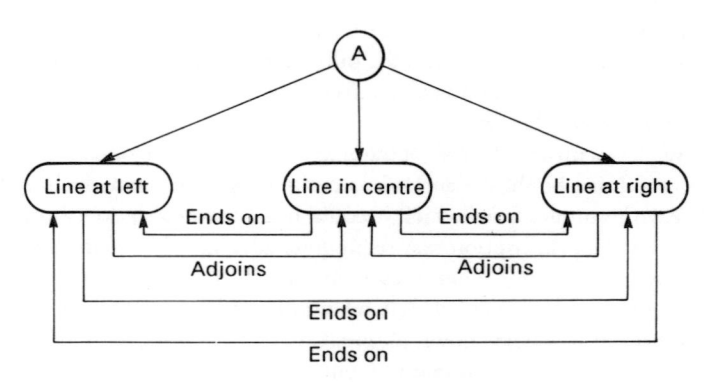

Figure 5.10 *Description of an A*

72

Knowledge and ways of obtaining it

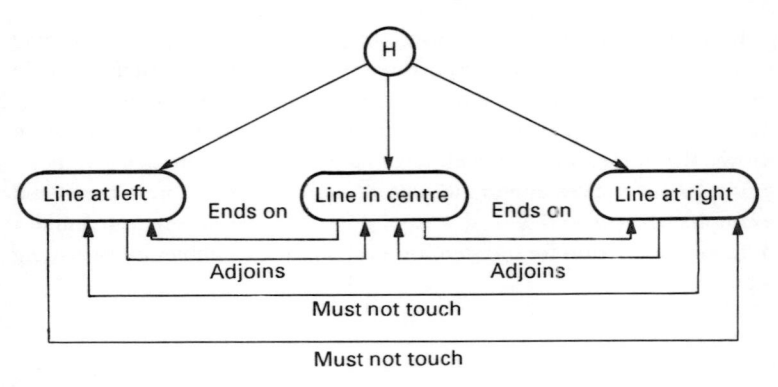

Figure 5.11 *Amended description of an H*

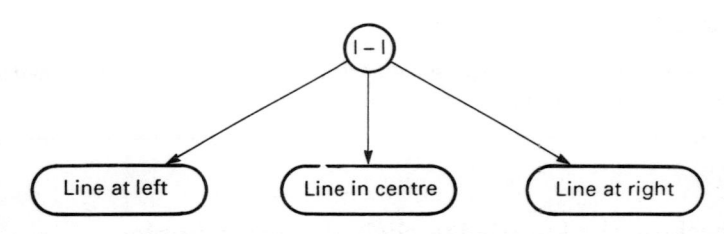

Figure 5.12 *Description of a broken H*

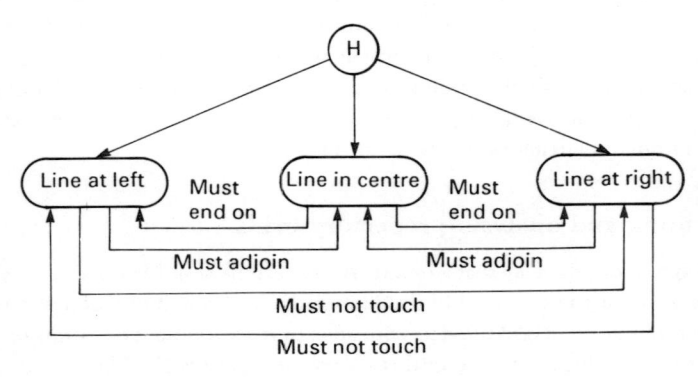

Figure 5.13 *Further amended description of an H*

73

In this way, the use of near misses strengthens the description by adding both forbidden and required aspects to the description. In a richer domain than that of this example, further instances of the concept to be recognized can be given in order to generalize the description. This illustration shows the importance of well-selected near misses: in general, good examples are equally important. The order in which the near misses and examples are presented is also important, for the system can build a different description for different orderings of the examples in its training set.

Question 2

Devise a training set for: (i) Q, (ii) P, (iii) F.

Question 3

Devise a system that, when presented with any three lines might be trained to recognize a triangle. Devise a training set for triangle recognition.

Checking the knowledge elicited from examples

Although knowledge may be elicited automatically from examples, the methods described in the previous two sections only allow for partial automation. An expert must generate the examples in the first place, may need to present them in an effective order, and must approve the knowledge that is elicited whatever form it may take. It may be necessary to repeat the cycle of generating examples, presenting them and examining the resulting knowledge before approval can be given. The full context of the automatic elicitation is shown in Figure 5.14.

Refining and analysing repertory grids

In this section, the way that a repertory grid can be simplified and analysed to make clear the structure of the knowledge contained in it is illustrated with reference to a grid filled in with an expert's assessment of a number of theatrical productions. The grid is shown in Figure 5.15. The maximum and minimum ratings for each construct are 10 and 1.

Knowledge and ways of obtaining it

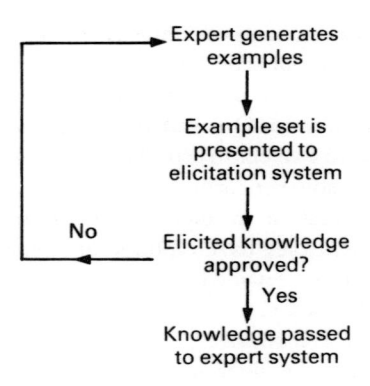

Figure 5.14 *The context of automatic elicitation from examples*

		E1	E2	E3	E4	E5	E6	E7	E8	
		Lettice and Lovage	*The Seagull*	*The Tempest*	*Two for the See-Saw*	*Tom Jones*	*Madame Bovary*	*A Midsummer Night's Dream*	*Kipling*	
C1	Good Production	7	7	7	7	5	4	2	9	Bad Production
C2	Well interpreted	6	7	8	5	6	4	5	9	Poorly interpreted
C3	Well acted	9	8	9	5	6	5	3	10	Poorly acted
C4	Gripping	7	7	8	4	5	3	2	10	Boring
C5	Strong response	9	7	9	3	5	1	6	10	Weak response
C6	Good costumes	6	7	7	5	5	5	3	9	Poor costumes
C7	Good stage set	7	6	4	7	6	3	7	9	Bad stage set
C8	Long	5	5	5	9	10	8	6	5	Short
C9	Full of ideas	5	6	7	6	5	3	5	8	Devoid of ideas
C10	Well written	4	8	10	5	5	2	9	10	Badly written

10 ← → 1

Figure 5.15 *A filled-in repertory grid*

75

Advanced Students' Guide to Expert Systems

The grid contains assessments of performances of eight plays: the assessments are based on a set of ten constructs. Each construct ought to be assessing some quite different aspect of the productions, and it is worth checking to see that they do. One way of doing this is by comparing the set of values assigned to two constructs, that is, by comparing two rows of the grid. If two rows show very little difference, they are manifestations of the same knowledge and one of them can be discarded, whereas if two rows are quite different they have captured different aspects of the situation and both should be retained. Similar rows indicate that one construct has been badly chosen, and dissimilar rows that the corresponding constructs have been well chosen.

One way of assessing the difference between two rows is to add up all the magnitudes of the differences between the corresponding values in each row. The magnitude of the difference of two numbers is the difference between them with the sign neglected. Thus, the magnitude of the difference between 8 and 5 is:

magnitude(8 − 5) = magnitude(3) = 3

and the magnitude of the difference between 2 and 6 is:

magnitude(2 − 6) = magnitude(− 4) = 4

Calculated in this way, the difference between the first two rows of the table is:

1 + 0 + 1 + 2 + 1 + 0 + 3 + 0 = 8

The maximum possible difference between two rows is (10 − 1) = 9 for each of the eight elements, giving 72. Two identical rows will have zero difference. Table 5.4 gives the differences between the value sets of all the constructs.

Table 5.4 *Differences between the value sets of all the constructs of Figure 5.15*

	C1	C2	C3	C4	C5	C6	C7	C8	C9	C10
C1	0	8	11	6	16	5	11	25	9	19
C2		0	9	8	12	5	11	23	7	13
C3			0	9	11	8	18	30	16	16
C4				0	10	7	15	31	11	15
C5					0	15	17	33	15	13
C6						0	14	24	8	16
C7							0	20	10	18
C8								0	20	32
C9									0	14
C10										0

Knowledge and ways of obtaining it

The smallest value in this table is 5, for the difference between both the pair C1 and C6 and the pair C2 and C6. This means that, in terms of this exercise, the pair of constructs good production–bad production and good costumes–bad costumes elicit much the same knowledge, as do the pair well interpreted–poorly interpreted and good costumes–bad costumes. This strongly suggests that the construct good costumes–bad costumes is unnecessary.

Other pairs of constructs with small differences are C1 and C4; C4 and C6; and C2 and C9. The difference in each case is less than ten per cent of the maximum possible difference. The two appearances of C4 (gripping – boring) indicate that it is hardly worth retaining, while C9 (full of ideas – devoid of ideas) differs so little from C2 (well interpreted–poorly interpreted) that it, too can be discarded.

In this way, the number of constructs can be reduced to seven, all of which differ by more than (an admittedly somewhat arbitrarily chosen) ten per cent. The resulting reduced grid is shown in Figure 5.16.

Now, it is possible to analyse the reduced grid, to bring the knowledge

		\multicolumn{8}{c}{Productions}	
		E1	E2	E3	E4	E5	E6	E7	E8	
		Lettice and Lovage	*The Seagull*	*The Tempest*	*Two for the See-Saw*	*Tom Jones*	*Madame Bovary*	*A Midsummer Night's Dream*	*Kipling*	
C1	Good production	7	7	7	7	5	4	2	9	Bad production
C2	Well interpreted	6	7	8	5	6	4	5	9	Poorly interpreted
C3	Well acted	9	8	9	5	6	5	3	10	Poorly acted
C5	Strong response	9	7	9	3	5	1	6	10	Weak response
C7	Good stage set	7	6	4	7	6	3	7	9	Bad stage set
C8	Long	5	5	5	9	10	8	6	5	Short
C10	Well written	4	8	10	5	5	2	9	10	Badly written

Figure 5.16 *Reduced repertory grid*

Advanced Students' Guide to Expert Systems

it contains into better focus. One way of doing this is to measure the similarity between the value sets of the various elements of the grid (the productions) so as to be able to group together those that are most similar. The degree of similarity between two productions can be calculated in the following way:

1. Calculate the difference between the two columns corresponding to the two productions by adding the magnitudes of the differences of corresponding entries, as described above
2. Calculate the percentage similarity from 100 − 100 × difference/(7 × 9).

(Notice that the maximum value for the difference is 7 × 9 because 9 is the span from the maximum to the minimum value of a construct, and a column contains 7 such values. When the difference is at its maximum, the percentage similarity is zero. On the other hand, if the difference is zero, then the formula gives the similarity as 100%.) The similarity between E1 and E2 can be calculated thus. The difference between them is:

$$0 + 1 + 1 + 2 + 1 + 0 + 4 = 9$$

while the similarity is:

$$100 - 100 \times 9/(7 \times 9)$$
$$= 100 - 100/7 = 86\%$$

Table 5.5 *Percentage similarities of the elements of Figure 5.16*

	E1	E2	E3	E4	E5	E6	E7	E8
E1	100	86	83	75	75	59	67	77
E2		100	88	74	77	58	75	78
E3			100	61	64	51	66	85
E4				100	88	78	74	54
E5					100	75	74	54
E6						100	64	35
E7							100	59
E8								100

Table 5.5 gives the percentage similarities of the elements. This table can be used to show the way that similar elements form clusters. From the numbers in the table, a tree of the kind shown in Figure 5.17 can be drawn; from the tree, the clusters that exist at a given level of similarity can be read. The tree is drawn by using the following rules:

Knowledge and ways of obtaining it

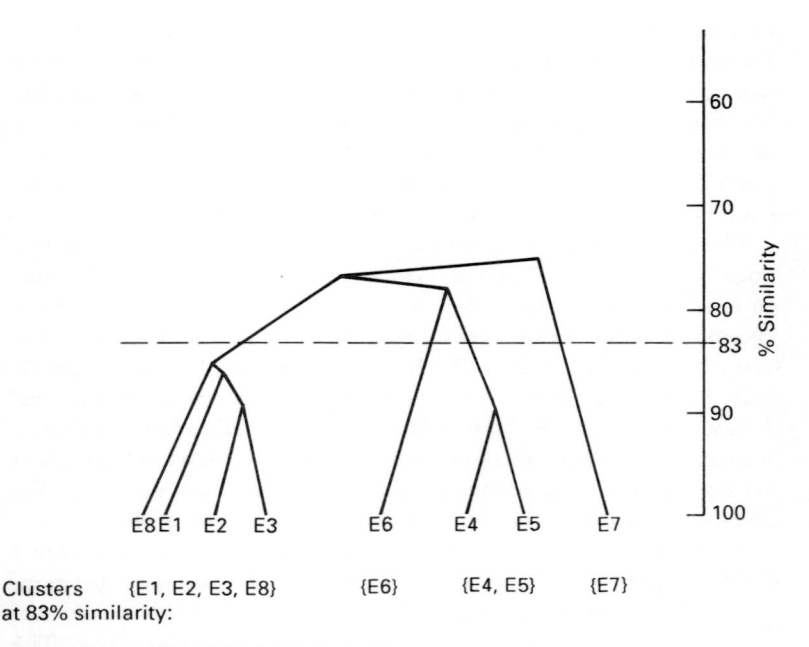

```
                                            ─┤60


                                            ─┤70
                                                   %
                                                   Similarity
                                            ─┤80
                                            ─ 83
                         ─ ─ ─ ─ ─ ─ ─ ─ ─ ─ ─
                                            ─┤90


                                            ─┘100
    E8 E1  E2   E3    E6    E4   E5    E7
```

Clusters   {E1, E2, E3, E8}   {E6}   {E4, E5}   {E7}
at 83% similarity:

Figure 5.17 *The clusters in the grid*

1 Find the largest number in the table that has not already been considered
2 Read off the elements labelling the row and the column of the number, and take the appropriate action from the following –
   ● if neither element is in a cluster, start a cluster with these elements
   ● if one of the elements is already in a cluster and the other is not, add the second element to that cluster
   ● if the elements are in separate clusters, join the clusters
   ● if both elements are in the same cluster, do nothing
   ● repeat from beginning until all the elements are in one cluster.

Figure 5.17 is constructed by starting with the 88 for E2 and E3, which puts these two elements in a cluster with a similarity of 88%. The 88 for E4 and E5 causes exactly the same thing to be done for them. The next highest number is 86 for E1 and E2: E2 is already in a cluster, and so E1 is added to it at the 86% level. The 85 for E3 and E8 causes E8 to be added to the cluster that already contains E1, E2 and E3. After this, the 78 for E4 and E6 adds E6 to the cluster with E4 and E5 in it. At this point, there are

79

Advanced Students' Guide to Expert Systems

two clusters: one contains E1, E2, E3 and E8, while the other has in it E4, E5 and E6. There is another 78 for E2 and E8, but they are already in the same group, so nothing happens. There are two 77s. One is for E1 and E8, but they are already in the same group. The other is for E2 and E5, which are in different clusters and so the clusters are joined at the 77% level. Finally, among the 75s is the one for E7 and E2, which joins E7 to the cluster containing all the other elements, and completes the tree.

When the tree has been drawn, we can read from it the answer to a question such as the following: 'Which productions were markedly similar to each other?' In Figure 5.17 a line drawn at a level of 83% similarity cuts the ends of the branches of the tree to leave the answer to the question as the clusters containing E1, E2, E3 and E8; E6 only; E4 and E5; and E7 only. Expressed in English, this means that the productions of *Lettice and Lovage*, *The Seagull*, *The Tempest* and *Kipling* were all markedly similar, as were the productions of *Two for the See-Saw* and *Tom Jones*. At the chosen level of similarity, neither the production of *Madame Bovary* nor that of *A Midsummer Night's Dream* were markedly similar to any of the others.

To summarize, methods have been presented to show that, given a filled-in repertory grid, it is possible to carry out two kinds of operations on it. The constructs can be examined to determine which are essential and which are not, so that any that are redundant may be removed. The elements can be compared and any that are similar can be placed in clusters. By these means, the grid can be refined and analysed to expose aspects of the knowledge it contains.

Assignment 5

1 Devise the skeleton for a repertory grid for recording knowledge of television programmes by finding an appropriate set of constructs. Choose some television programmes as the elements for the grid, and then fill in the grid. Reduce the grid if necessary and then analyse it.

2 Use the same set of television programmes as the basis for constructing a table of examples. Classify each programme as 'worth watching' or 'not worth watching'. Choose, say, three attributes shared by the programmes and complete the table with the values of the attributes and the classifications. Refine the knowledge in the table to gain a set of rules.

3 Examine the results of stages 1 and 2 to see if they display any agreements or disagreements. If there are any, then explain them. If any disagreements exist, check that there are no conflicts between the knowledge originally recorded in the grid and the table.

Knowledge and ways of obtaining it

Recap

- the process of extracting and externalizing the knowledge of an expert is known as knowledge elicitation. The process of fixing that knowledge in a form that can be stored and manipulated by a computer-based system is known as knowledge acquisition. A necessary step between the two processes is the expression of the elicited knowledge in a readily comprehensible form
- the techniques for eliciting knowledge from an expert include interviewing, the compilation of sets of examples for subsequent analysis, problem solving and methods based on psychological theories
- knowledge can also be elicited by methods that can be automated. This is particularly desirable in view of the labour-intensive nature of the methods listed above
- methods for the automatic elicitation of knowledge include the refinement of tabulated examples and the analysis of repertory grids.

Answers to questions

1 The refined knowledge is expressed by the rules:
 IF colour = red and texture = rough THEN class = unappealing
 IF colour = blue or (colour = red and texture = smooth) THEN class = appealing.
2 (i) near-misses could be O and G (ii) near-misses could include R, I and a reversed C (iii) near-misses could include E, T rotated 90 degrees anti-clockwise and an inverted L.
3 A system similar to the one for recognizing capital letters would suffice. Good near-misses for a triangle would be two lines in a 'V' shape; three lines making three of the sides of a quadrilateral; and four lines, three of which formed a triangle.

6: Knowledge representation and inference

Objectives

After reading this chapter, you should be able to:
- list the requirements of any worthwhile knowledge representation scheme
- list the knowledge representation schemes that have been used in practice
- explain how knowledge is represented when using rules, semantic nets, logic and frames
- represent knowledge by using these schemes
- choose the scheme that is most appropriate to represent knowledge in specific circumstances
- explain how inference works when using each of the representation schemes.

Scenario

'Dr Newman looks very worried these days.'

'Yes, and so would you if you'd had someone at you for weeks on end trying to find out what's inside your head and, what's worse, succeeding.'

'Well, now you've got his expertise out of him, I suppose you're ready to tip it into your expert system shell. As it happens, I know someone ...'

'It's alright, thankyou, and I'm familiar with the jargon now. I've found a knowledge engineer myself.'

Elicited knowledge is recorded in a way that is suitable for people to examine and understand it. Before it can constitute a knowledge base that is suitable for a computer, it must be represented in a way that suits the computer. A good representation for structured knowledge should have the following properties:

Knowledge representation and inference

- representational adequacy. It should support the acquisition of all the aspects of the knowledge in all their subtlety
- representational efficiency. It should allow efficient acquisition so that the knowledge is stored compactly and is easily accessible
- inferential adequacy. It should be possible to use the knowledge in any way that may be appropriate
- inferential efficiency. The knowledge should be located and used rapidly and without the need of excessive computation

Only a small number of schemes have been used to represent knowledge, in practice. The most common are:

- rules – knowledge representation is, perhaps, usually associated with rules, but they do not necessarily always provide the most appropriate representation
- semantic nets – in providing a pictorial representation that is equivalent to a formal description, semantic nets can be easily appreciated
- logic – mathematical logic can be used as a formal description language with the advantage that well-known mathematical techniques can then be brought to bear
- frames – this scheme draws to some extent on the others.

This chapter first describes these representation schemes, and then considers how they are used.

Knowledge representation schemes
Rules

Knowledge can be represented with rules of the general form:

>IF condition THEN action

with a condition that, in specific circumstances, is either true or false, and an action to be carried out only when the condition is true. The condition and action can both be composed of several parts. A rule could be written as:

>IF condition – 1
>AND condition – 2
>AND condition – 3
>THEN action – 1
>AND action – 2

Advanced Students' Guide to Expert Systems

to indicate that only if all the conditions are satisfied should both actions be taken. A rule can also be written:

    IF condition − 1
    OR condition − 2
    OR condition − 3
    THEN action − 1
    AND action − 2

to indicate that all the actions should be taken if any one of the conditions is true. A rule of this kind is equivalent to a simpler set of rules, in this case to:

    IF condition − 1
    THEN action − 1
    AND action − 2
    IF condition − 2
    THEN action − 1
    AND action − 2
    IF condition − 3
    THEN action − 1
    AND action − 2

To give an illustration of a rule from a typical rule-based expert system, one of *MYCIN*'s rules (see Chapter 7) may be written as:

> IF the stain of the organism is gramneg
> AND the morphology of the organism is rod
> AND the aerobicity of the organism is aerobic
> THEN there is strongly suggestive evidence that the class of the organism is enterobacteriaceae

A small knowledge base consisting of knowledge represented by rules is given in Figure 6.1. The knowledge is concerned with what particular types of people should wear. This example illustrates that knowledge can be structured into modules. The knowledge base can be expanded simply by adding more rules, so that a system drawing on this knowledge base can be given access to more knowledge, and so can expand its capabilities, without requiring any change to the system itself.

It is possible to have rules that describe what to do with other rules, so introducing knowledge of a higher level. One way of doing this is to introduce a number of possible modes that the system may assume during its operation. Then rules such as:

Knowledge representation and inference

Dress rules:
Rule 1   If the person is serious
             and the person lives in the South
             then the person should wear a jacket
Rule 2   If the person is an academic
             and the person is socially active
             and the person is serious
             then the person should wear a jacket and bow tie
Rule 3   If the person lives in the South
             and the person is an academic
             then the person should wear a tie
Rule 4   If the person is an industrialist
             and the person is socially active
             then the person should wear a jacket but not a tie

Location rules:
Rule 5   If the person lives south of Watford
             then the person lives in the South

Social rules:
Rule 6   If the person is an industrialist
             and the person is married
             then the person is socially active
Rule 7   If the person is an academic
             and the person is married
             then the person is serious

Profession rules:
Rule 8   If the person works in a university
             or the person teaches in a college
             then the person is an academic
Rule 9   If the person works for a company or the person is self-employed
             then the person is an industrialist

Figure 6.1   *A small knowledge base composed of rules*

    IF condition
    THEN action
    AND mode is 2

can set the system to one of its modes. Other rules of the form:

    IF mode is 3
    AND condition – 1
    THEN action – 1

only apply when the system is in a particular mode. A rule of the first kind has been used to decide which subset of rules of the second kind will subsequently be applicable.

Advanced Students' Guide to Expert Systems

To summarize this section, we can say that when knowledge is represented by rules:

- 'chunks' of knowledge can be organized into modular form
- knowledge can be added to a knowledge base in a straightforward way by adding rules to it
- rules about rules provide a way of supplying higher-level knowledge.

Activity

Your work station is attached to an electronic mail network. All messages passed by the system have a header with the following fields:

    To: From: Copies to: Subject: Date:

Entering *anyone* in the *copies to*: field causes a copy to be sent to anyone on the network, so creating 'electronic junk mail'.

Write a set of rules to filter out the mail you want to receive and to delete the rest. The work station can take the following actions: *delete* an item of mail, *move to* one of the folders named Urgent, Pending and Interesting an item of mail, *show* an item as soon as it arrives. A rule could be:

    IF from: My Boss and Date: today THEN show

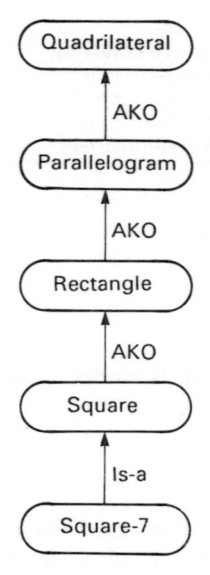

```
        ┌──────────────┐
        │ Quadrilateral│
        └──────────────┘
               ▲
               │ AKO
        ┌──────────────┐
        │ Parallelogram│
        └──────────────┘
               ▲
               │ AKO
        ┌──────────────┐
        │  Rectangle   │
        └──────────────┘
               ▲
               │ AKO
        ┌──────────────┐
        │    Square    │
        └──────────────┘
               ▲
               │ Is-a
        ┌──────────────┐
        │   Square-7   │
        └──────────────┘
```

Figure 6.2 *A simple semantic net*

Knowledge representation and inference

Semantic nets

Semantic nets are well-suited for representing knowledge of a hierarchical nature. Figure 6.2 illustrates a representation of this kind for geometrical knowledge: the nodes in the diagram represent geometrical objects and sets of objects. The *is – a* label on an arc indicates that the object from which the arc originates is a member of the set to which the arc leads. An *AKO* (for *a kind of*) link indicates that the set from which the arc originates is a sub-set of the set to which the arc leads. For this reason, an *is – a* link is always found at the beginning of a chain of *AKO* links, as with the particular square at a given location on a computer screen which is a square, which is a kind of rectangle, which is a kind of quadrilateral, and so on.

The net of Figure 6.2 can be extended in the way illustrated by Figure 6.3 to include properties of the objects represented by nodes. The arc label *has–prop* denotes that the object from which the arc originates has the property to which the arc points, while *n–sides* denotes that the object has the number of sides to which the arc leads. Figure 6.3 serves to introduce the important idea of *inheritance*. As a particular square is an instance of the class of all squares, it naturally has all the attributes of that class. The general

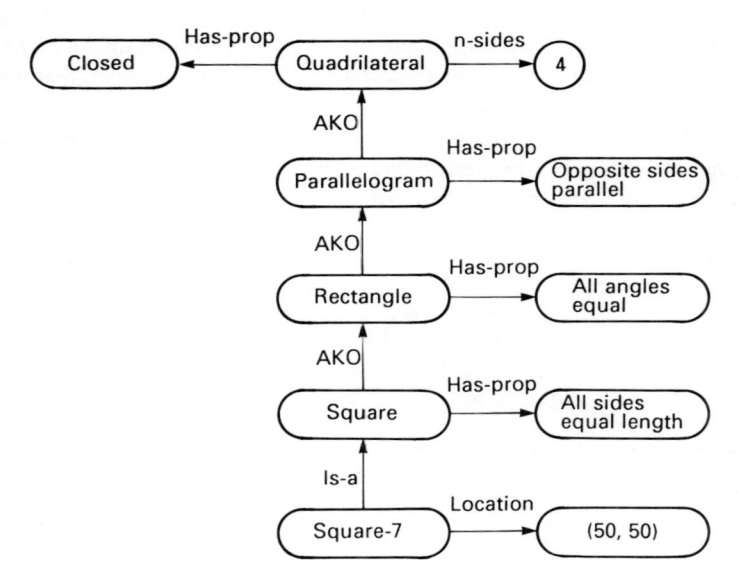

Figure 6.3 *An elaboration of Figure 6.2*

Advanced Students' Guide to Expert Systems

attributes of a square do not have to be attached to every instance of a square, but can be inherited from the class. This means that some of the attributes of a particular object can be found by moving up the *is – a* link from that object to the object representing its class and taking its attributes. The property that a square has *all sides equal* can be inherited in this way. The attributes that give a specific square its individuality, such as its location and size, must still be attached to it locally. An object can also inherit attributes from any set joined to it by a chain composed of an *is – a* link and any number of *AKO* links, because moving further up this chain leads to less restrictive, and so larger, sets to which the object belongs. In this way, a specific square can inherit properties from the class of rectangle, parallelograms, and so on.

The idea of a *default* value is also supported by semantic nets. Suppose that a particular computer graphics application displays many coloured shapes, but nearly all the squares are red. In this case, it would be worth attaching the property that squares are red to the set of squares, as shown in Figure 6.4. This ensures that all squares are red unless something is done about it, that is, they are red by default. If one particular square is green, then that attribute can be attached directly to it, as in Figure 6.4, and then its colour does not have to be inherited.

Another area where semantic nets are eminently suitable is in recording the way in which objects are made up of their component parts as, for example, in computer-aided manufacturing. The reason is, again, that the structure of the knowledge is hierarchical. Figure 6.5 shows the way that knowledge about how a bicycle is composed of its various parts might be represented. The *is – part* link indicates both that an individual component is part of a sub-assembly and that a sub-assembly is part of the whole. This representation can also be enriched, as shown in Figure 6.6, by relating objects to their classes and by attaching properties to objects.

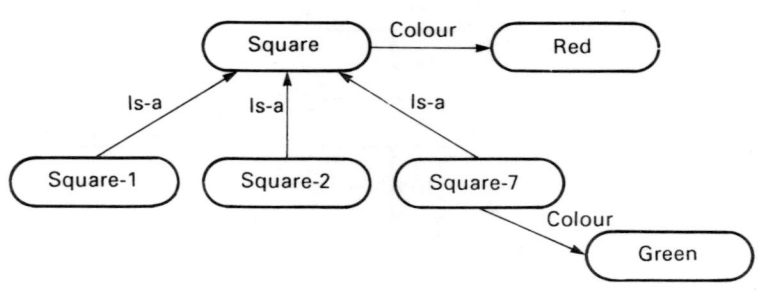

Figure 6.4 *An attribute value set by default*

Knowledge representation and inference

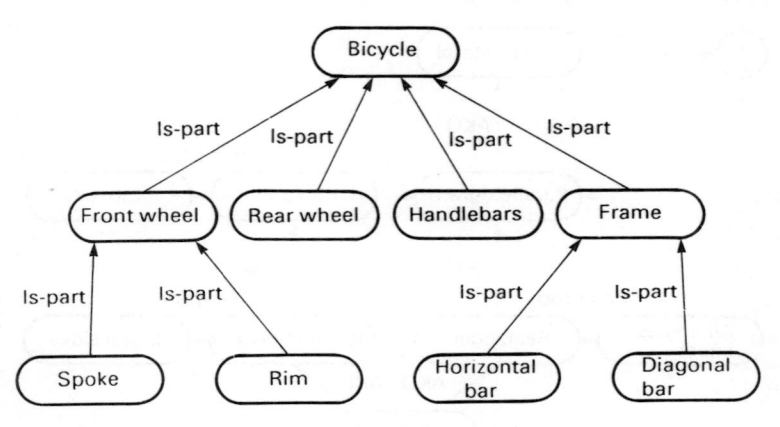

Figure 6.5 *A semantic net for components parts*

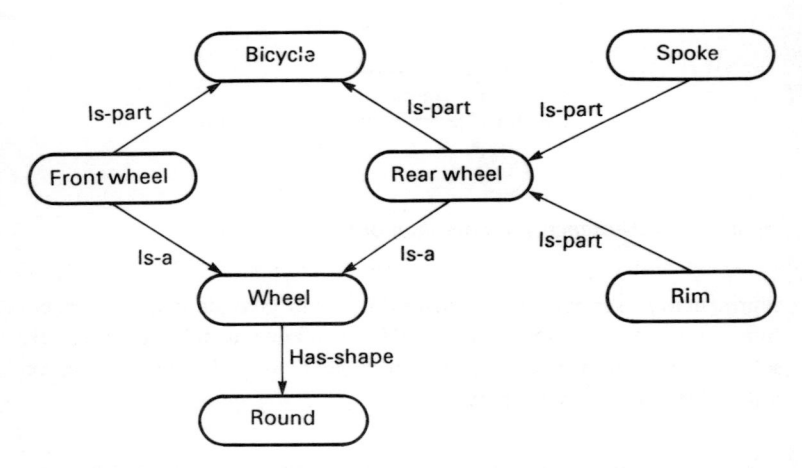

Figure 6.6 *An elaboration of a component-part net*

Figure 6.7 demonstrates that attributes can be inherited from more than one chain of links. Clearly, the attributes inherited from one chain should not contradict those from another. It may be necessary to collect attributes from all the chains to get a complete description of the object, but in many cases a complete description may not be necessary. The real value of multiple chains of inheritance is that one of them may carry all the attributes that are needed in a particular case. In this way, the form of

Advanced Students' Guide to Expert Systems

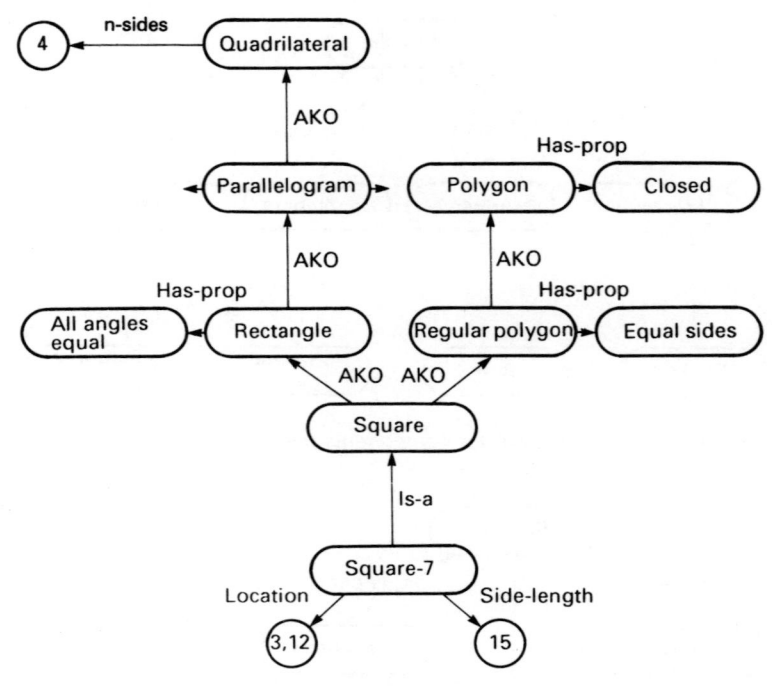

Figure 6.7 *Inheritance via more than one path*

representation supported by semantic nets can give alternative perspectives on an object, each of which will be suitable at different times. By selecting the appropriate chain, an object can be placed in a given context with all the necessary properties.

Activity

Devise a semantic net to represent the activity of visiting a restaurant for a meal. The nodes should represent the states of the activity, starting with *enter the restaurant*, and should include, among others, *order the wine* and *pay the bill*. The main links will be labelled *follows*, as in *State 3 follows State 2*. Give each state suitable attributes, and allow for some of the states to be by-passed (so that there is no compulsion to have a sweet if you have already eaten too much!).

Knowledge representation and inference

Logic

Knowledge of an object can be represented by describing what is known to be true about it with correctly formed sentences of logic. Thus, a large, red block which is known as *block-11* can be represented by the sentence:

block(block-11) AND large(block-11) AND red(block-11)

Knowledge about an environment can be represented by describing each object in the environment in this way, and also the relations between objects. The environment of Figure 6.8 can be represented by the sentences:

block(a)
block(b)
block(c)
on(a, table)
on(c, table)
on(b, c)

Thirdly, knowledge about an event can be represented by something that alters the description of one environment to that of another.

If we concentrate for the moment on the representation of an environment, it is possible to check such a representation for consistency, that is, to ensure that it contains no sentences, or parts of sentences, contradicting each other. The representation just given for the environment of Figure

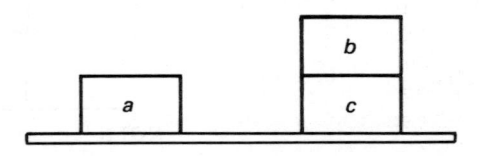

Figure 6.8 *An arrangement of the blocks world*

Advanced Students' Guide to Expert Systems

6.8 is rather too simple to illustrate how this may be done, so consider the following description, which will be referred to as *Description 1*:

> An environment contains three blocks identified as a, b and c. Block a is cubical and red; block b is cylindrical or red (or both); block c is cylindrical or green (or both). Block a is on block c, which is red. If block c is on block b then b is cubical.

This can be represented by the logical sentences:

cube(a) AND red(a)
cylinder(b) OR red(b)
cylinder(c) OR green(c)
on(a, c) AND red(c)
IF on(c, b) THEN cube(b)

This set of sentences is tested for consistency by replacing each of the sentences by simpler sentences to build a *tableau*. The replacement rules are shown in Figure 6.9. The complex sentences may be simplified in any order; it makes matters simpler to deal with the sentences containing AND first, in which case the tableau begins with:

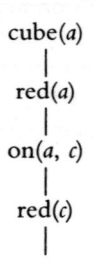

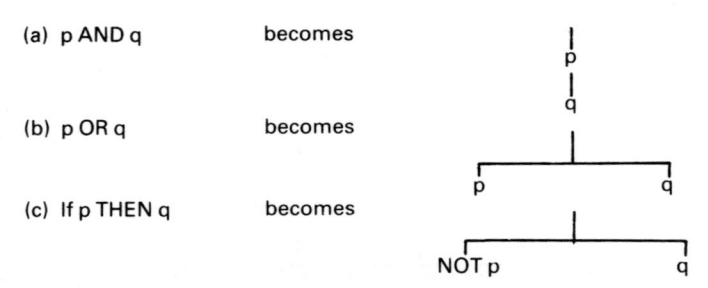

cube(a)
|
red(a)
|
on(a, c)
|
red(c)
|

(a) p AND q   becomes   p
                                      |
                                      q

(b) p OR q   becomes   ┌──┴──┐
                                   p   q

(c) If p THEN q   becomes   ┌──┴──┐
                                 NOT p q

Figure 6.9   Replacement rules

Knowledge representation and inference

The sentences containing OR can be dealt with next to give:

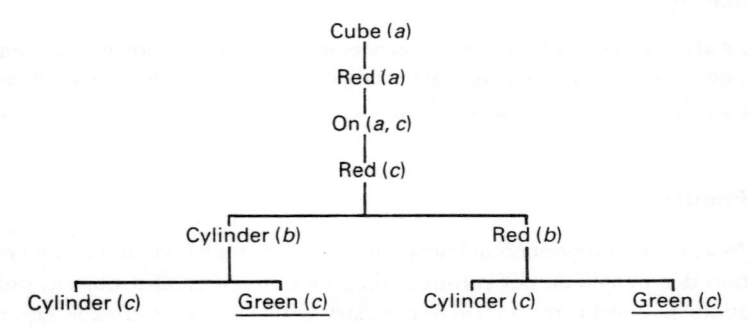

```
                    Cube (a)
                       |
                    Red (a)
                       |
                    On (a, c)
                       |
                    Red (c)
                    /       \
            Cylinder (b)    Red (b)
            /      \         /      \
    Cylinder(c) Green(c) Cylinder(c) Green(c)
```

This tableau has four branches. The two that are underlined contain contradictions by declaring that block c is both red and green, and so they can be closed. The other two branches represent situations in which no contradictions have occurred so far. Adding the simplified sentences to replace the *IF – THEN* sentence gives the completed tableau of Figure 6.10. One of the remaining branches contains a contradiction by declaring that block *b* is both a cube and a cylinder. The other three branches describe situations in which the set of sentences representing the situation can all be true. For this reason, the set of sentences is consistent. A set of sentences is inconsistent when all the branches of the corresponding tableau contain inconsistencies so that there is no situation in which all the sentences can be true at the same time.

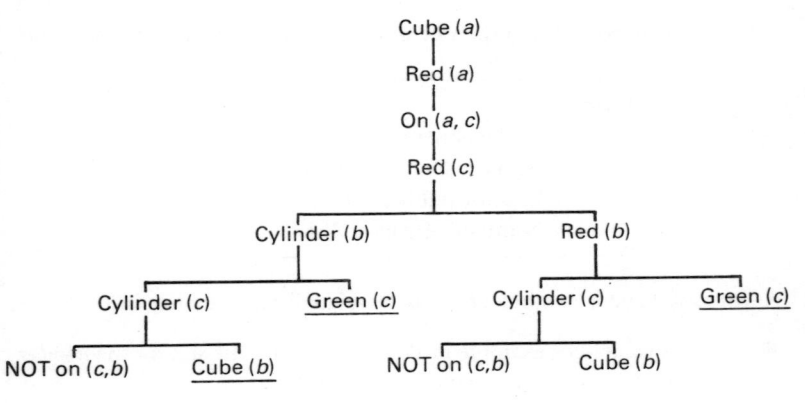

```
                         Cube (a)
                            |
                         Red (a)
                            |
                         On (a, c)
                            |
                         Red (c)
                         /       \
                 Cylinder (b)    Red (b)
                  /      \         /      \
         Cylinder(c) Green(c) Cylinder(c) Green(c)
           /     \                /     \
   NOT on(c,b) Cube(b)     NOT on(c,b) Cube(b)
```

Figure 6.10 *The completed tableau*

Advanced Students' Guide to Expert Systems

Activity

Read from Figure 6.10 the circumstances in which the situation is consistent. Check the circumstances against the original description of the environment.

Frames

As a means of representing knowledge, the frame is based on the observation that people do not construct their ideas about familiar objects, situations and events from scratch, but carry with them a set of expectations about these things. A frame represents an object or situation by describing the collection of attributes that it possesses. It does this by listing all the attributes of a typical case, and by providing a slot for each. This description of the typical case can then be used to capture any individual case by placing the values of its attributes in the respective slots.

To illustrate, books in general might for some purposes be adequately described by the frame structure:

> *Book*
> Title:
> Author:
> Date of publication:
> Number of pages:

Any particular book could then be described by filling in each slot, as in:

> *Book*
> Title: Nineteen Eighty-Four
> Author: George Orwell
> Date of publication: 1949
> Number of pages: 251

A slot may have a number of facets associated with it, such as:

- a default value. For example in a frame for *chairs*, the slot for the *number of legs* might well have a default value of 4
- a range of permitted values for the slot

Knowledge representation and inference

- a procedure for filling the slot. A frame for a rectangle could have slots for its length, breadth and area. The area slot could contain a procedure to determine when the length and breadth slots had been filled so that it could then fill the slot with their product.

A slot can also be filled in other ways:

- with a link to another frame from which it inherits values
- with a link to a frame for an object that is near to but not quite the same as the object represented by the frame. A frame for a cup might, for example, be linked to one for a jug
- with a link to a frame representing an object that would commonly accompany the object represented by the frame. For example, a frame for a cup might be linked to a frame for a saucer

This list suggests that a frame becomes a more powerful means of knowledge representation when it is incorporated in a network of frames. The network can place an individual frame within a broad structure of knowledge, can support inheritance and can make simple the location of associated knowledge.

Most of these possibilities are illustrated in the next example which gives a frame to represent a cup. The frame has a number of slots, each with one or more facets. By filling the slots, a specific cup may be represented. The *if needed* facet contains a procedure for filling the slot: the name of the procedure begins with a per cent sign and is either %*ask*, which asks the user for the required value and accepts a response, or a formula to be evaluated. On the other hand, if the object in question is not a cup but is something similar, the frame can direct attention to likely alternatives such as a jug or a basin. The frame is:

Cup
  is–a: crockery
  shape:
        Value set: round and dished and handle
                          octagonal and dished and handle
        Default: round and dished and handle
        If needed: %ask
  use:
        Value set: drinking, collecting, decoration
        Default: drinking
        If needed: %ask

size:
           Value set: height from 1 inch to 4 inches

volume:
           Default: 1/3 pint
           If needed: %(height 3/18)

status:
           Value set: OK, broken, chipped, antique
           If needed: %(if not(smooth rim) then chipped)
                                  %(if age >100 then antique)

near miss:
           No handle □→ *basin* frame
           Height too great □→ *jug* frame

association:
           □→ *saucer* frame

Activity

Devise a structure for a frame to keep a reference to any book or article in a journal that you have read on the subject of expert systems. Include slots for *near miss* and *association* links so that the reference frames are joined in a network. This will make it easier to track down a particular reference in those annoying circumstances when you cannot quite remember it.

Inference

The second part of this chapter examines ways of connecting existing knowledge to create new knowledge when using each of the representation schemes. We shall see that rules can be chained together, paths in a network can be activated, logical inferences can be drawn from given clauses, and that frames can have their slots filled as well having paths to other frames activated.

Rules

New knowledge can be created by chaining rules together. From the fact that A is true and the rule *IF A THEN B*, we may deduce that B is true. After this, the existence of a rule such as *IF B THEN C* allows us to deduce

Knowledge representation and inference

that C is true. This process can be continued for as long as the rules will connect. The process is known as *forward chaining* because it uses rules in a chain to move forward from given knowledge to new knowledge. The chain may be represented by:

<u>A
IF A THEN B</u>
    <u>B
    IF B THEN C</u>
            C

The process may be illustrated by using the set of rules of Figure 6.1 to find how a married and self-employed person should dress. The requirement gives the starting facts:

the person is self-employed
the person is married

Now rules can be invoked by scanning the list until one is found with a condition part that matches one or more of these facts, and the process continued until one of the *dress* rules (rules 1 to 4) is reached to give the advice as to how this person should dress. The first rule to match is rule 9. This allows the extra knowledge that:

the person is an industrialist

to be added to the initial facts. Scanning the list again shows a match at rule 6 giving:

the person is socially active

Scanning again gives a match at rule 4, which is one of the *dress* rules, so that the procedure can stop with the advice that:

the person should wear a jacket but not a tie

Forward chaining is equivalent to finding what can be inferred from given knowledge by using a set of rules. It is possible to chain rules in the opposite direction (backward chaining), and this is equivalent to asking the question: 'Can this assertion be proved from the facts at our disposal?' In other words, we set out to find if C is true. A rule such as *IF B THEN C*, asserts that C is true if B is also true. A rule *IF A THEN B* asserts in turn that B is true if A is. If A is a known fact, then the chain is complete and C is shown to be true.

Backward chaining can be illustrated by using the set of rules in Figure

97

6.1 to determine what sort of a person should wear a jacket. Thus starting with:

> the person should wear a jacket

the first rule to give a match in its conclusion part is rule 1. This asserts that:

> the person is serious
> the person lives in the south

Rule 7 matches the first of these assertions, giving the set:

> the person is an academic
> the person is married
> the person lives in the south

Rule 8 now gives:

> the person works in a university OR the person teaches in a college
> the person is married
> the person lives in the south

Finally, Rule 5 leaves:

> the person works in a university OR the person teaches in a college
> the person is married
> the person lives south of Watford

As no more rules match, these facts describe the sort of person who should wear a jacket.

The smallness of the set of rules in Figure 6.1 obscures certain difficulties that may arise with larger sets. It may be that at any point there is more than one rule that matches the requirement to continue the chain. In this case some means of resolving the conflict must be invoked. The simple expedient of taking the first matching rule to be encountered is employed in some systems, but others employ more sophisticated strategies. Another matter that arises is how to decide when to use forward chaining and when to use backward chaining. In general, this can be decided by examining the branching factor of the chaining process and deciding which is the smaller of the number of new facts that can be determined from the given ones, and the number of ways in which an assertion can be demonstrated to be true in terms of the given facts.

Knowledge representation and inference

Activity

Determine from the rule base in Figure 6.1 what a person working in a university south of Watford should wear, and who should wear a jacket and a bow tie.

Semantic nets

When an object can be associated with a node in a semantic net, that node can be marked and paths to and from it can be traced in order to recall knowledge associated with the object. By tracing chains consisting of an *is – a* link and *AKO* links, properties that are inherited by the object can be found and contexts can be established. Links associated with attributes can be traced to determine attribute values.

In the semantic network shown in Figure 6.7, when the square named *Square – 7* is marked, the properties it inherits in the context of four-sided figures can be found by tracing the path towards the *quadrilateral* node, and the properties inherited in the context of closed figures by tracing the links leading towards the *polygon* node. The values of its size and position attributes can be found by tracing the corresponding attribute links.

In fact, a semantic network is equivalent to a particular form of description expressed in logic. The fact that two linked nodes are equivalent to a logical clause expressing a relationship between two objects means that a semantic network is equivalent to a logical description in which all the clauses express a relationship between two objects.

Logical clauses relating more than two objects can be transformed to a set of clauses each of which expresses a relationship between two objects. This can be illustrated by considering how the sentence: 'Nancy played Greensleeves on the flute on Sunday' may be represented. First, it can be written as a logical clause relating four objects:

played(Nancy, Greensleeves, flute, Sunday)

Then it can be written, using the name 'Musical-event-12' for the event, as the following set of simple clauses:

player(Nancy, Musical-event-12)
played(Greensleeves, Musical-event-12)
instrument(flute, Musical-event-12)
time(Sunday, Musical-event-12)
is – a(Musical-event-12, recital)

Advanced Students' Guide to Expert Systems

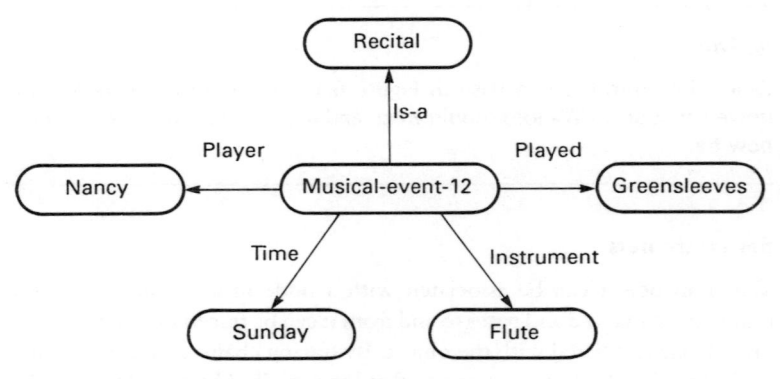

Figure 6.11 *Semantic net for an event*

From this, the semantic net representation of Figure 6.11 can be drawn at once. The different forms of representation illustrate the way that any logical description can be converted to a semantic net.

In practice, semantic nets have been used as a form of implementation for logical descriptions. One reason for this is that their pictorial form makes them much easier to understand and to check than a list of logical clauses.

Logic

A form of inference that is widely used with logic is known as *resolution*. The basic resolution rule is this:

Two clauses of the form

A OR B
(NOT B) OR C

may be resolved to give

A OR C

In effect, the B and (NOT B) terms clash to cancel each other out. The rule holds because if B is false then A must be true to make the first clause true, whereas if B is true then C must be true to make the second clause true. Consequently, when the original clauses are both true the clause A OR C must always be true.

It is worth noting that as special cases the pair of clauses A OR B and

Knowledge representation and inference

(NOT B) resolve to A; the pair A OR B and (NOT A) resolve to B; and A and NOT A resolve to leave nothing.

Resolution is applicable to logical clauses in general because of the existence of transformation rules that ensure that any logical clause can be re-written so that it involves no logical operators other than NOT and OR. We have already met these rules in one form during the course of the tableau method: for the purposes of resolution, they take the form:

> the clause A AND B is re-written as the two clauses A and B
> the clause IF A THEN B is re-written as the clause (NOT A) OR B

In addition, the general laws of logic can be invoked to allow:

> NOT (NOT A) to be re-written as A
> NOT(A AND B) to be re-written as (NOT A) OR (NOT B)

With this background, the idea of inference by resolution can be explained. The basic situation is that given a consistent set of logical clauses, we want to infer the truth of a further clause. For instance, from a set of clauses describing a particular situation, we might want to infer the truth of some further statement about the situation, or from a set of clauses describing a problem we could test a further statement purporting to be the solution of the problem to see if it were true. One way to proceed (and probably the obvious one) would be to form a new set of clauses by adding the clause to be inferred to the given set, and then to demonstrate the consistency of the new set. In fact, it turns out to be simpler to form a new set by adding the *negation* of the clause to be inferred to the given set, and then to demonstrate that the new set is *not* consistent. This method of demonstrating the truth of an assertion by showing that its negation cannot be true is called *proof by refutation*.

We will give an example to show how the method works, and then discuss the merits of the method. Suppose that in the situation represented earlier in the chapter by *Description 1*, we want to demonstrate the truth of the statement: 'C is a cylinder'. First, we have the clauses of the description, which are:

> cube(a) AND red(a)
> cylinder(b) OR red(b)
> cylinder(c) OR green(c)
> on(a, c) AND red(c)
> IF on(c, b) THEN cube(b)

To these, we need to add the common-sense knowledge that a block

101

Advanced Students' Guide to Expert Systems

cannot be both a cube and a cylinder, and that it can only be one colour. This gives the clauses:

NOT(cube(X) AND cylinder(X))
NOT(red(X) AND green(X))

The variable X has been introduced to save writing out the first clause three times, once for *a* (to say that it cannot be both a cube and a cylinder), again for *b* and again for *c*. The name of a variable is distinguished from that of an object by denoting it by a capital letter. A variable can be set to an instance of an object, so that in this case, X can be set to *a*, *b* or *c*. The clauses of the given set now need to be rewritten, and this gives:

cube(*a*)
red(*a*)
cylinder(*b*) OR red(*b*)
cylinder(*c*) OR green(*c*)
on(*a*, *c*)
red(*c*)
NOT(on(*c*, *b*)) OR cube(*b*)
NOT(cube(X)) OR NOT (cylinder(X))
NOT(red(X)) OR NOT(green(X))

To this set, we must add the negation of the clause we wish to infer, which is:

NOT(cylinder(c))

Now we can resolve this last clause with the fourth clause of the given set, cylinder(*c*) OR green(*c*), to get green(*c*). This result can be resolved with the last clause of the given set, NOT(red(X)) OR NOT(green(X)), after setting X to *c*, to give NOT(red(*c*)). Finally, this can be placed against the sixth clause of the set, red(*c*), to reveal a contradiction – it is not possible for *c* to be red at the same time as *c* is not red. (An alternative way of saying the same thing is that the clauses red(*c*) and NOT(red(*c*)) resolve to give a nil result which indicates a contradiction.) The resolution steps can be traced in the diagrammatic form shown in Figure 6.12.

If we use the method to try to show that the block *c* is green, the chain of resolutions shown in Figure 6.13 results. It halts after obtaining NOT(cube(*c*)) with no further resolution possible. Thus, no contradiction has been established, and so the truth of the assertion has not been demonstrated.

The reason that it is preferable to infer the truth of an assertion by

Knowledge representation and inference

```
NOT (cylinder (c))        cylinder (c) OR green (c)
     |                   /
  green (c)              NOT (red (X)) OR NOT (green (X))
     |                         | X = c
     |                   NOT (red (c)) OR NOT (green (c))
  NOT (red (c))           red (c)
     |
 contradiction
```

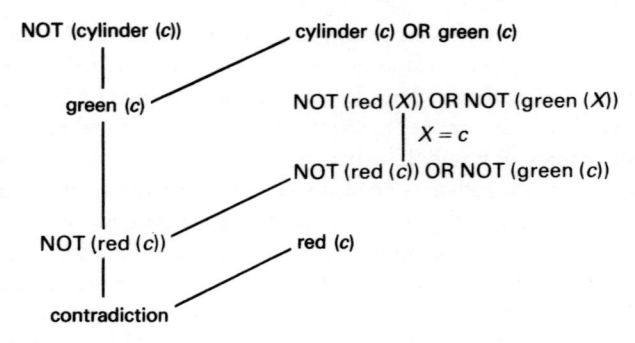

Figure 6.12 *Resolution to show that* c *is a cylinder*

```
NOT (green (c))       cylinder (c) OR green (c)
     |               /
  cylinder (c)        NOT (cylinder (X)) OR NOT (cube (X))
     |                      | X = c
     |               NOT (cylinder (c)) OR NOT (cube (c))
  NOT (cube )c))
```

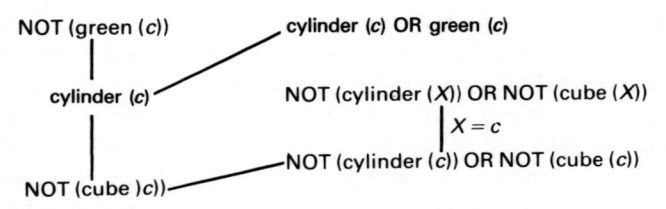

Figure 6.13 *Resolution, trying to show that* c *is green*

resolution rather than by, say, simply searching forward from the given clauses in the hope of eventually happening on a proof, is that the negated clause provides a starting point for the inference while, at each stage, finding a clause that will resolve provides a way of continuing. Resolution will demonstrate the truth of an assertion that is true, but if the assertion is false the method may, as we have seen, or may not halt.

Activity

Make sure that you understand exactly why the resolution tree shown in Figure 6.13 has not proved that c *is green*.

Frames

The initial problem when using frames is to select the appropriate frame for the task in hand. For example, when a robot vision system is attempt-

Advanced Students' Guide to Expert Systems

ing to identify an object on a table-top, the frame for a cup might be selected in preference to that for a saucer, jug or plate on the basis of some small amount of evidence. The choice of frame may then be confirmed as further slots are filled or the 'near-miss' slots may be brought into use to revise the choice of frame. If a change to a near-miss becomes necessary, knowledge already gathered need not be scrapped: the contents of slots filled on the basis that the object is a cup may be used to fill the corresponding slots if the object subsequently turns out to be a jug.

With the appropriate frame selected, the slots in that frame list expectations about the object, and can direct the knowledge-gathering process. Facts that have not been observed can be sought. The fact that a cup should have a handle may be inferred even if the handle is not visible from the current point of view. Facts of this kind do not rely on the context (a cup always has a handle) but because one frame forms part of a network, contextual information can be gathered via links to other frames. Contexts can be established and values inherited via *is-a* and *AKO* links.

In broad terms, inference with frames is similar to that with semantic nets, but is enhanced by the fact that the frame is a structured object representing a chunk of knowledge. The slots of a frame correspond to expectations about an object, and relieve the system of the chore of having to find out about the object from scratch every time. As part of a network, the frame allows initial choices to be changed readily, contexts to be established and inheritance to take place.

Activity

Describe the methods of inference that would be employed with the knowledge representations of the first, second and fourth activities in this chapter.

Assignment 6

Having elicited the knowledge of an expert lecturer in assignment 5, this assignment requires you to choose a means of representation suitable for acquiring this knowledge for a computer-based teaching system. The system can have access to a knowledge base acquired for an expert system for the material it is to teach, but it will also need a teaching knowledge base if it is to be able to teach that knowledge in an expert way.

Knowledge representation and inference

Consider the following factors in reaching a decision on which form of representation to use. The knowledge will naturally fall into 'chunks'. For example, the lecturer will have a set of formal teaching methods as well as informal ones, and will know when to use them. There will be knowledge about the knowledge. The lecturer will know when to use simple words to express the knowledge to be taught, and when the knowledge can be taught without regard to the complexity of the language used. The teacher will look for cues to trigger certain approaches to teaching. A formal presentation may change abruptly to an attempt to stimulate the student if boredom appears to be setting in. If the student is suffering from a misconception, the lecturer will attempt to correct it. If necessary knowledge has not been learnt, or has been forgotten, the teacher will provide it. The form of representation chosen must be able adequately to represent and support these, and other, factors.

Recap

- to be useful, a knowledge representation scheme must provide a means of representing knowledge that is both adequate and efficient. It must also allow for adequate and efficient inference mechanisms
- the knowledge representation schemes that have been used in practice are: rules, semantic nets, logic and frames
- when knowledge is represented as rules, inference takes place by chaining rules together. Forward chaining starts from known facts and repeatedly invokes rules whose condition-part is rendered true to establish new facts. Backward chaining seeks to prove a statement corresponding to the right-hand side of a rule true by repeatedly attempting to determine whether the condition parts of rules are true
- semantic nets consist of nodes to represent items of knowledge and links that represent relations between them. Particular types of links, most notably *is–a* and *AKO* links, support inheritance and the provision of default values. Inference takes place by the activation of nodes once the items to which they correspond have been observed, and of the chains of links to them
- logical clauses can be used to represent knowledge. When this is done, a method known as *resolution* provides an efficient inference mechanism. A representation in logic can be converted to a semantic net, and the pictorial nature of the net can make it a helpful complementary description.

Advanced Students' Guide to Expert Systems

- a frame represents a chunk of knowledge by collecting together the attributes of an item of knowledge. Each attribute is assigned a slot which can be filled with the value of the attribute. The attribute slots represent expectations about the item in question. A frame can have further slots to hold pointers to other frames, so that a network of frames can be established. This allows inheritance and the provision of default values in the same way as with semantic nets. Inference takes place by filling the slots of a frame and by activating the frames and paths in a network of frames.

7: Some expert systems

Objectives

By reading this chapter you should:
- gain an appreciation of how the knowledge representation schemes of the previous chapter, and their associated means of inference, have been incorporated in existing expert systems
- gain an appreciation of the ways in which the basic expert system architecture has been elaborated in recent systems.

Various expert systems are presented in this chapter. The architecture of each, that is, its structure and organization, is described first followed by its mode of operation. The architecture corresponds to the static organization of the system, and the mode of operation to its dynamic behaviour. In the first part three classic expert systems are covered to show how the knowledge representation schemes described in the previous chapter, and the associated inference mechanisms, have been implemented in practice. The second part deals with expert systems with more innovative architectures: the systems themselves are either newly developed or still in the course of development. The general form for the architecture of an expert system has been shown in Figure 2.16. The architectures of these systems illustrate some of the ways that the basic architecture can be developed.

Classic systems

The architectures and modes of operation of three classic expert systems are described in this section to show how practical systems have been based, respectively, on rules, semantic nets and frames.

MYCIN

MYCIN is a consultant expert system that asks questions, makes diagnoses and then offers advice to clinicians treating patients who are suffering

Advanced Students' Guide to Expert Systems

from blood infections. It can diagnose certain kinds of antimicrobial infections and recommend the appropriate drugs to treat them. The work on *MYCIN* began at Stanford University in 1972 and the most prominent of the researchers contributing to it was E Shortliffe.

MYCIN is a rule-based expert system, and it operates primarily by backward chaining. The structure of the inference is that it proceeds from patient to disease to treatment. The description that follows is intended to convey the bare essentials of the system and of the way that it operates. The system is in fact a good deal more elaborate than the description suggests, but to include the detail of all the elaborations would be to obscure the simplicity of the underlying core.

The basic architecture of *MYCIN* consists of:

- a collection of facts about the patient whose condition is to be diagnosed. The facts come from the patient's medical record, and may also be acquired during the consultation with the system
- a knowledge base containing a collection of rules. The rules are mainly concerned with diagnosis and treatment, but there are also rules to determine how the others are selected and some that are concerned with how information is gathered from the consultant using the system
- a collection of utility procedures. These are for purposes such as gathering information, indicating when information can be obtained

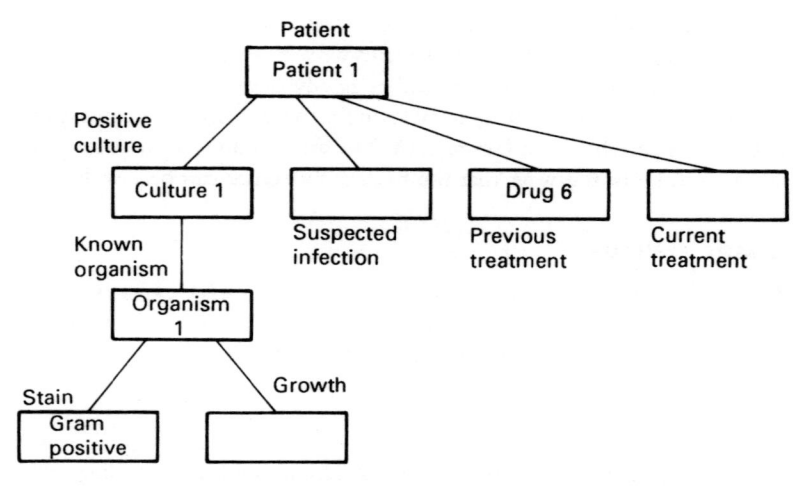

Figure 7.1 *A context tree for a patient*

Some expert systems

only by carrying out a laboratory test, and for selecting the rules that are candidates for chaining.
- an inference engine that carries out the backward chaining.

The facts about the patient are recorded in the form of a tree as shown in Figure 7.1. The root of the tree is identified with the patient. Facts are recorded in the form of object-attribute-value triples. The attributes of a patient can include cultures that have proved positive, suspected infection, previous treatment and current treatment. Thus, one triple in the figure is *patient 1 − culture 1 − organism 1*. The tree can be continued to deeper levels because, for example, *organism 1* can have attributes, such as *stain*, which in turn can take a value such as *gram positive*. (Incidentally, the value of *stain* would have to be determined by a laboratory test.)

The point of storing the facts about the patient in the form of a tree is that each branch leading from the root is separate from all the others, and can be regarded as a context. The act of finding a fact automatically establishes a context, the purpose of which is to concentrate the area of activity of the inference engine by restricting its choice of rules for chaining to those that apply in that context.

The knowledge base contains some 450 rules. Each one takes the usual form:

IF condition THEN action

although the condition part can consist of several tests ANDed together. A typical rule is:

IF   the stain of the organism is gram positive
AND the morphology of the organism is coccus
AND the growth conformation of the organism is chains
THEN there is suggestive evidence that the identity of the organism is streptococcus

Note that the three tests in the condition part all refer to the value of an attribute of an organism, and that the conclusion relates to the identity of the organism. The conclusion is not, however, a definite one, reflecting the fact that medical diagnosis is not always an exact matter, but one that deals with uncertainties, probabilities and incomplete knowledge.

The utility procedures include:

- LABDATA, to indicate that the result of a test or condition can be found only by carrying out an experiment in the laboratory, and not, for example, by asking the patient. It also indicates to the physician consulting *MYCIN* that a laboratory test is required

Advanced Students' Guide to Expert Systems

- UPDATED-BY, a facility to determine all the rules that are candidates for chaining to the current rule. It finds all the rules in the current context that mention the condition part (or the test from it that is presently under consideration) of the current rule in their action part
- FINDOUT, a mechanism for gathering information to evaluate the condition part of the rule under consideration. If the information is available, it prevents the system from asking for it again. If the information is not available, it invokes, as appropriate, either UPDATED-BY, to determine the further rules needed to evaluate the condition, or LABDATA.

The inference engine starts with the rule:
    IF   there is an organism that requires treatment
    AND   consideration has been given to the possible existence of additional organisms requiring therapy
    THEN compile a list of possible treatments and find the best treatment in the list

It then proceeds, by backward chaining, to determine if the tests in the condition part are true, so that only if there is an organism requiring treatment and if other possibilities have been covered is the action part of the rule carried out and a list of possible treatments constructed. The backward chaining repeatedly invokes rules relating conclusions to evidence until facts about the patient are invoked to give values to the clinical attributes. This establishes a context in which a diagnosis can be made. Following this, the action part of the initial rule can be carried out to determine the possible treatments.

The chaining of the rules is controlled by the procedure named MONITOR, the structure of which is given in Figure 7.2. MONITOR makes use of FINDOUT: its structure is shown in Figure 7.3. Note that FINDOUT invokes MONITOR so that there is mutual recursion between the two procedures. FINDOUT is always called from MONITOR so that its RETURNs always cause a return to MONITOR. Apart from its initial call, MONITOR is called by FINDOUT, and its RETURNs cause a return to FINDOUT. The initial call to MONITOR is made in the attempt to carry out the initial rule. If the final RETURN from MONITOR is the one following *reject the rule*, the condition part of the rule is false, and no further action takes place. When the final RETURN is the one following *add the conclusion of the rule to the context tree*, the condition part of the rule is true, and the action part can proceed in the light of the established context.

Some expert systems

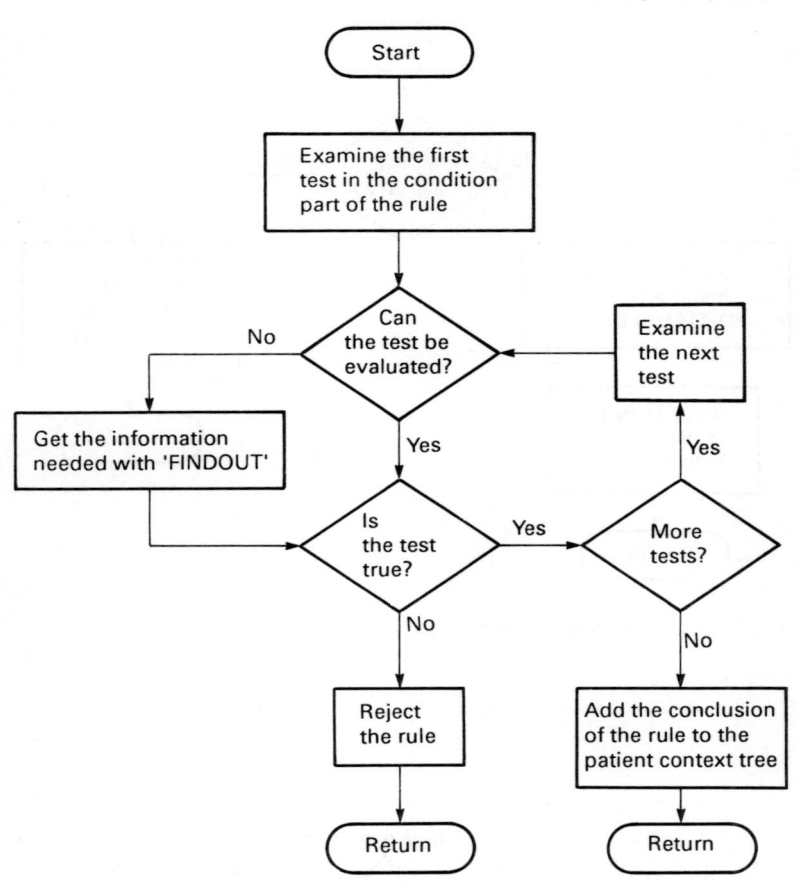

Figure 7.2 *The structure of MYCIN's MONITOR*

The rule-chaining mechanism also creates a tree: an illustration is shown in Figure 7.4. The initial rule is *MYCIN*'s rule 092. The first test of its condition part chains to rules 090 and 149, and either of these can give rise to a branch. Again, rule 090 can chain to several other rules, and this brings the possibility of further branches. The condition part of rule 149 contains three tests, and all of them must succeed before it is shown to be true. The second test in the condition part of rule 092 causes a similar development.

Advanced Students' Guide to Expert Systems

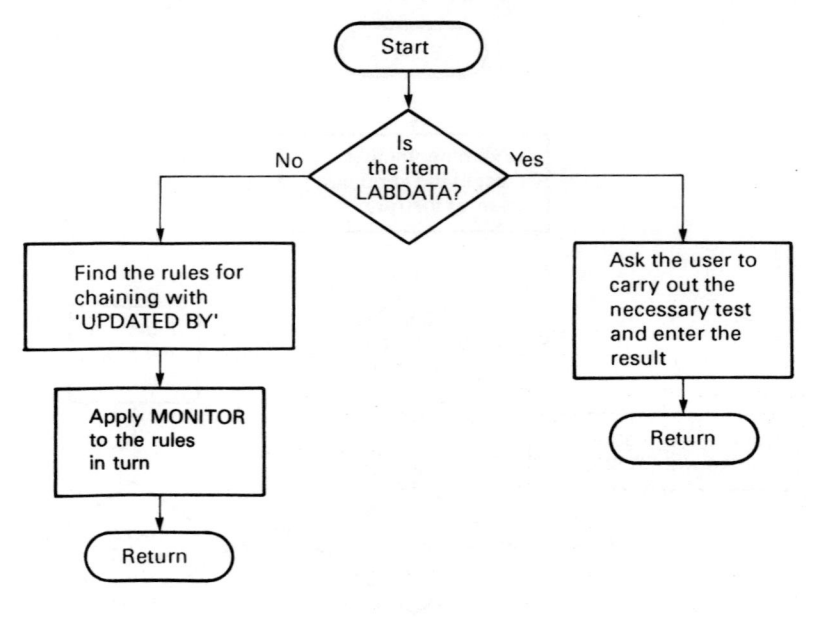

Figure 7.3 *The structure of MYCIN's FINDOUT*

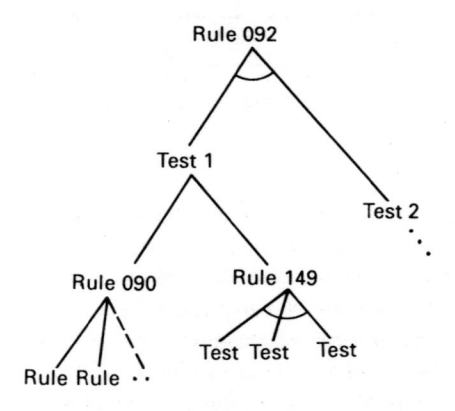

Figure 7.4 *Part of a tree showing MYCIN's rule-chaining*

Some expert systems

Most rule-based systems, whether backward- or forward-chaining, operate on principles similar to those embedded in the MONITOR and FINDOUT procedures. This applies equally to fully-fledged systems running on large computers and expert system shells for microcomputers. The predominance of rule-based systems has led to their identification with expert systems but, as we shall see in the following examples, other means of knowledge representation can be used and may, in certain circumstances, prove more suitable.

CASNET

CASNET is a consultant expert system for use in medicine. Its original application was to the diagnosis and treatment of disorders of the eye such as glaucoma. It deals with the same sort of knowledge as *MYCIN*, but it represents that knowledge in a quite different way. The system was developed by Kulikowski and Weiss starting in the early 1970s at Rutgers University.

CASNET represents its knowledge by a semantic network. The structure of the inference is to proceed from observations of the patient to disease states to disease category to treatment recommendations. A disease state is not in itself a disease but is a state of impairment or malfunction that is suffered during the course of a disease. To illustrate, lumpy glands do not in themselves correspond to mumps, but they are the obvious feature of one of the states that a patient with mumps passes through. The use of disease states implies that *CASNET*, and systems with the same architecture, can be applied to the diagnosis and treatment of diseases whose mechanisms are thoroughly understood in the sense that the pattern of states through which they pass is well known.

CASNET separates its factual knowledge into four groupings, or *planes*. They are:

- Observations, which can be symptoms, signs (sets of symptoms) or the results of tests
- disease states. These are linked in a network of their own to indicate the possible patterns of progress of the diseases that can be diagnosed by the system. There are initial states, representing the states from which a disease may start, intermediate states, and final states which, in general, represent the most serious stage of a disease. A path from an initial state to a final state traces one possible complete history of a disease, that is, the progress of a complete disease process. The form of a network of states on this plane is illustrated in Figure 7.5

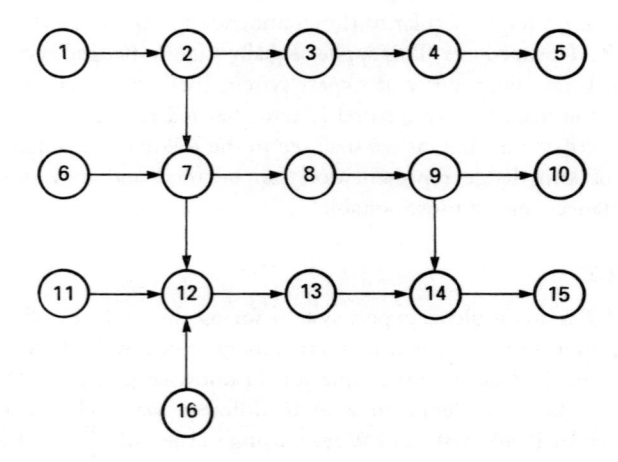

Figure 7.5 *A network of disease states*

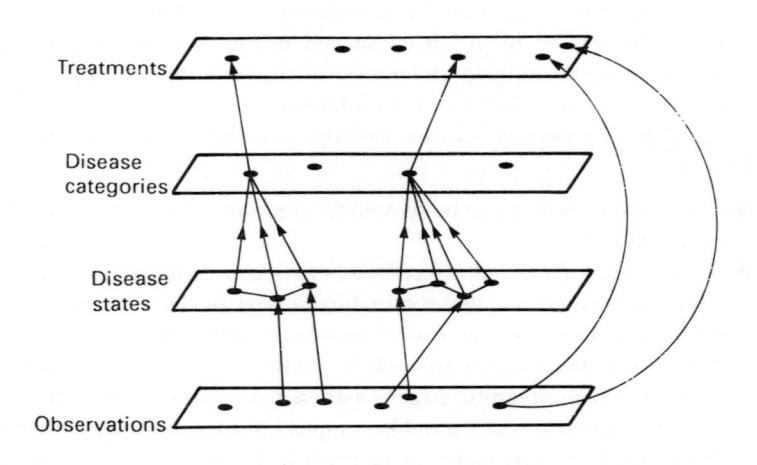

Figure 7.6 CASNET's *planes*

Some expert systems

- disease categories, to represent the classes of disease that can be diagnosed.
- treatments, corresponding to treatments for disease categories.

In addition, the planes are linked in the ways listed below to give the form of knowledge representation illustrated in Figure 7.6. There are links from:

- *observations to disease states*. These links are labelled with the degree of confidence that can be placed in the existence of the disease state when the observation has actually been made. The confidence factor can be positive to suggest that the disease state exists, and negative to suggest that it does not. A value of +1 indicates that the state is certain to exist, while a value of -1 indicates that it certainly does not exist
- *disease states to disease categories*. A link of this type goes from a set of disease states (which correspond to all or part of a disease process, or all or part of the history of the development of a disease) to a disease category. A link from a complete set of states, consisting of an initial state, a final state and all the states in between, would lead to a disease category corresponding to an established disease. The set of states on a path from an initial state only as far as an intermediate state could be linked to a category corresponding to something less than a full-blown disease
- *disease categories to treatments*. Each disease category is linked directly to its treatment
- *observations to treatments*. These links are less vital to the general structure of the architecture than the others, but observations can suggest treatments directly or, as important, can indicate a treatment that should not be given.

The inference process begins by taking the known observations about a patient, be they symptoms described by the patient or the results of tests on the patient, and using them to activate nodes in the plane of observations. In turn, this activates the links from those nodes. At this stage, various nodes in the plane of disease states are pointed to and so become candidates for activation. The fate of each candidate among the disease state nodes is determined in this way:

1 the degrees of certainty are read from the links pointing to the node, and the degree with the greatest magnitude is found. (Remember, the degree of certainty can take a value from +1 to −1. The magnitude of +0.6 is 0.6. The magnitude of −0.7 is 0.7)

115

Advanced Students' Guide to Expert Systems

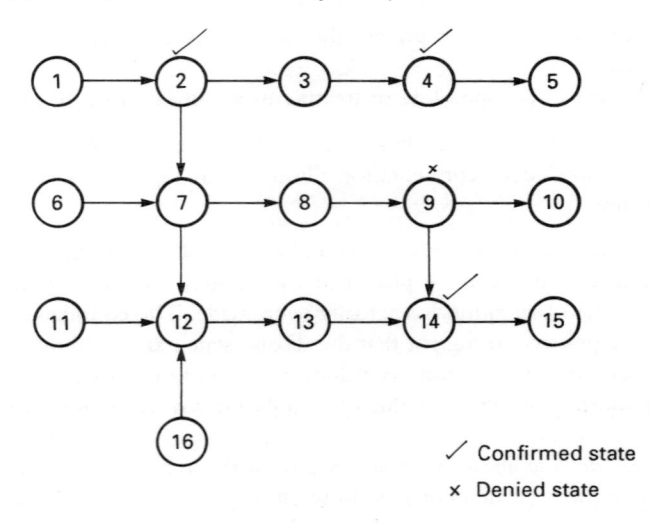

Figure 7.7 *The plane of disease states during inference with confirmed, denied and undetermined states*

2 if the selected degree of certainty exceeds a certain value (let us say, for the sake of illustration, 0.8) the disease state is confirmed. This means that the disease state is found to be present in the patient
3 if the degree of certainty falls below a second value (say -0.8) the disease state is denied. This means that the patient is not suffering the disease state
4 for other values of the degree of certainty, the disease state remains undetermined, meaning that there is insufficient evidence to decide whether the disease state is present in the patient.

At this stage, the plane of disease states could appear as shown in Figure 7.7. The next task is to determine possible paths in the plane that correspond to part or all of a disease process. These paths are the ones that begin from an un-denied starting state, contain no denied state, have at least one confirmed state, and finish on a confirmed state. Thus, the possible paths in Figure 7.7 are (1, 2); (1, 2, 3, 4); (1, 2, 7, 12, 13, 14); (6, 7, 12, 13, 14); (11, 12, 13, 14); and (16, 12, 13, 14).

Having found a path containing a set of disease states, the set will activate a path to a disease category which in turn will activate a path to a

Some expert systems

treatment recommendation. Finally, any activated links from the plane of observations and the plane of recommendations must be taken into account to supplement or modify the recommended treatment. The state of the knowledge structure at the end of the inference process can be illustrated schematically in the way shown in Figure 7.8.

The preceding description has been given in a way that assumes sufficient knowledge about the patient is available to trigger a treatment recommendation. If this is not the case, the condition of the plane of disease states suggests at once which nodes are the most promising candidates for confirmation. The confirmed states at the end of the paths are clearly supposed to describe the patient's current state: the states preceding them should therefore be states that the patient is still suffering, or has recently suffered. They are pointed to by the observations that can confirm or deny them, so the system can ask that these observations be made. In Figure 7.7 nodes 1, 3 and 13 are the next for investigation.

Besides directing the order in which observations should be made, another strength of *CASNET*'s knowledge representation is that it can be used to predict the next state of the patient's disease. This provides a means of confirming the diagnosis that has been made and also makes possible the taking of preventive measures.

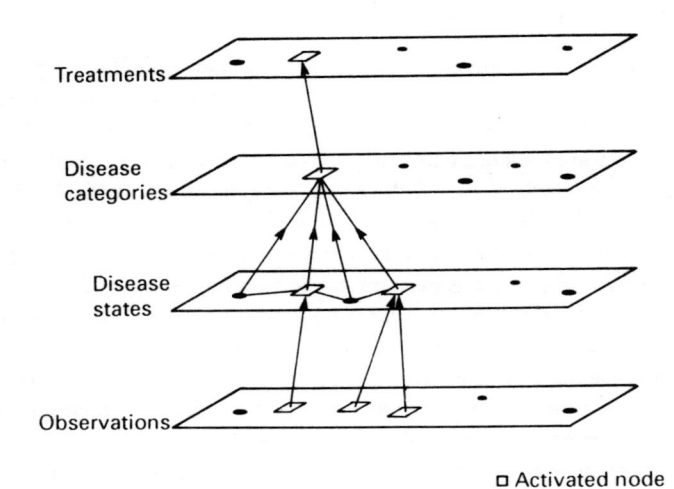

Figure 7.8 CASNET's *inference in action*

PIP

PIP was developed by Pauker and Szolovits at the Massachusetts Institute of Technology as a system for diagnosing the present illnesses of patients with kidney disorders. *PIP* uses frames for knowledge representation, and its inference mechanism relies on filling the slots of frames and taking advantage of the links joining the frames in a network.

The structure of *PIP*'s frame for a disorder is shown in Figure 7.9. The slots of the frame fall into five groups. These are for:

- typical and trigger findings. These slots are for information gathered about the patient that is typical of the disorder or is of the kind that would trigger an expert diagnostician to suspect the disorder
- confirmation and exclusion criteria. These slots are for information that is necessary definitely to confirm the presence of the disorder in the patient, or to rule it out
- complementary links. The pointers in these slots connect the frame to the frames for complementary diseases that are likely to be connected with the disorder in some way, or to be found accompanying it
- near-miss links. Links to disorders with similar symptoms and observations. These disorders might prove to be what the patient is suffering from if it turns out not to be the present one
- confirmation/denial estimator. These slots contain procedures for estimating the extent to which the disorder is or is not present

Initially, all frames are inactive. Inference begins by filling slots with information about the patient. A frame is activated when one of its trigger slots is filled. As soon as a frame is activated, all the frames to which it is joined by a complementary link are *semi-activated*, which means that they can be activated when one of their slots for typical information is filled instead of waiting for a trigger slot to be filled. Active frames can request that the information, if it is not already available, be gathered to fill their slots that are subject to assessment by the confirmation and exclusion criteria. The functions in the slots for confirmation/denial estimation can then be activated. If their estimate exceeds some pre-set threshold value, the frame will be confirmed: if it falls below a second threshold value, the frame will be denied. When the value lies between the two thresholds, the frame is returned to its original inactive state.

A confirmed frame becomes part of a hypothesis about the patient's condition, asserting that the patient has the disorder represented by the frame. The patient may also suffer from other disorders, and so any other

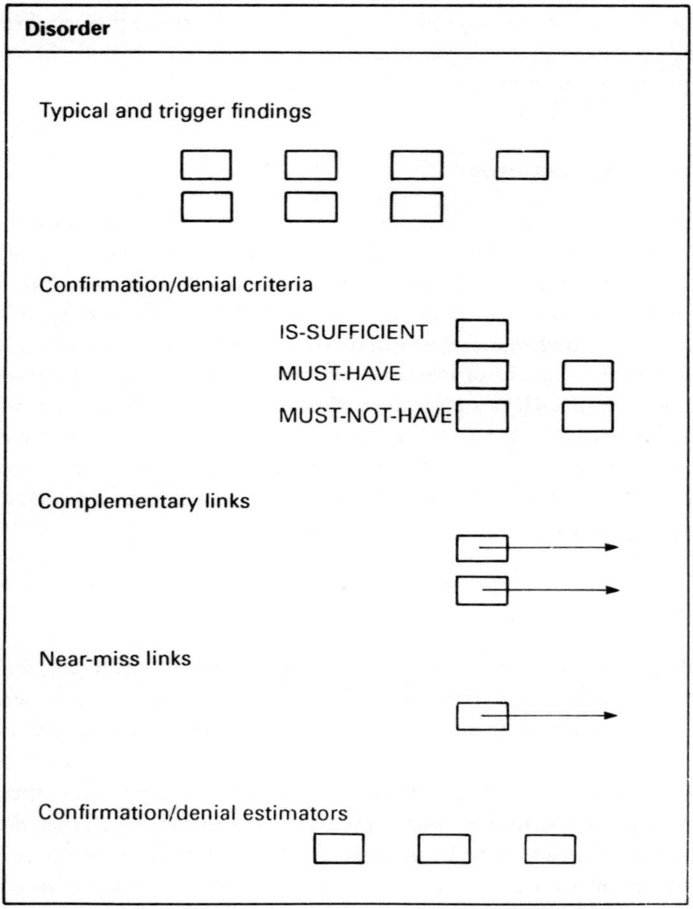

Some expert systems

Figure 7.9 PIP's frame organization

active frames will have to be investigated. A denied frame indicates that the patient is not suffering from the disorder associated with the frame: the frames to which it is connected by near-miss links are activated to determine if their diseases are present. When a frame is de-activated, a further round of information-gathering must take place, guided by the requirements of the unfilled slots in the frame.

The entire process continues until no more information is available or all the frames have been confirmed or denied. The final set of confirmed frames, joined together by their links, constitutes *PIP*'s hypothesis about the present state of the patient.

Some other systems

Three further systems are described in this section. The first and second, *IDM* and *CLINAID*, illustrate respectively innovative ways of extending the knowledge base and the architecture. The knowledge base of *IDM* is intended to capture expert knowledge more fully in that it contains not only expert knowledge in the form of 'tricks of the trade' but also a way of modelling the domain of expertise in detail so that the expertise can be explained. *CLINAID*'s architecture allows a collection of expert systems, each performing a sub-task, to co-operate in order to carry out one overall activity. The third example is *TK!Solver*, a well-known microcomputer program that adopts the conventional expert system organization in an interesting way.

IDM

IDM is a general expert system designed for diagnostic problem solving. Its performance is intended to model that of the human expert whose expertise consists of short cuts learnt from experience, but whose considerable experience allows him to explain the reason for the short cuts. To this end, *IDM* has a two-level knowledge base. One level contains the knowledge, in the form of short cuts and 'tricks of the trade', that allows the causes of problems to be diagnosed: the other enables the domain in which the problems occur to be modelled in detail. The benefits of the second, modelling, level are that detailed reasons can be given for any course of action recommended by the system; a problem presented to the system can be modelled to ensure that it really is a problem and not, for instance, an unusual but perfectly correct form of system behaviour; and the performance of the system can degrade gracefully towards the edges of its area of expertise rather than halting abruptly at some point.

The architecture of *IDM* is shown in Figure 7.10. It has two knowledge bases, each with its own inference engine, and an overall inference engine to determine which of the subsidiary engines to select. The so-called *experiential knowledge base* consists of a semantic network similar to that of

Some expert systems

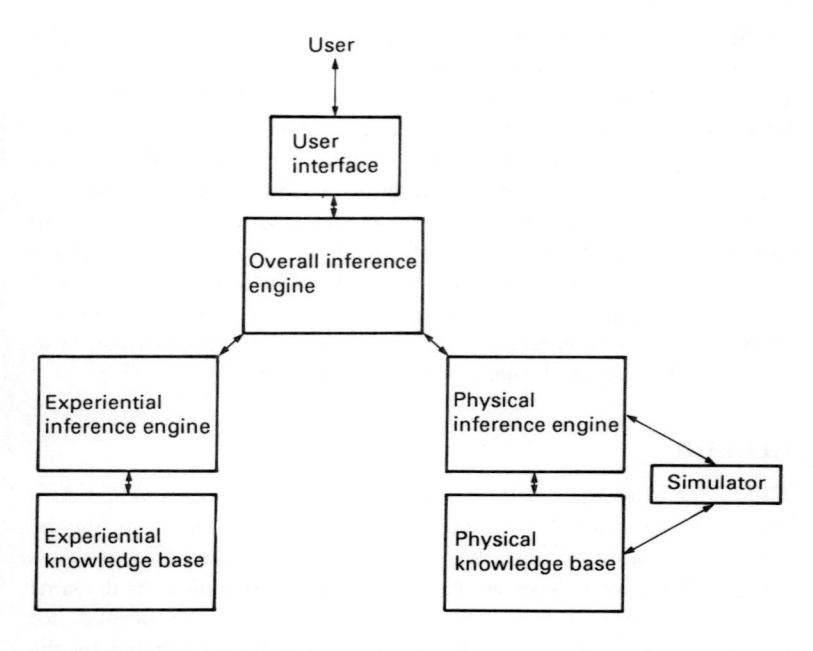

Figure 7.10 *The architecture of* IDM

CASNET and a frame system in which the frames are for entry points to the semantic network. The semantic network has three planes: one for observations, one for possible problem solutions and one for courses of remedial action. Each frame has slots relating to the nature of the problems that the system can tackle, and a means of confirming the frame. The *physical knowledge base* contains a set of basic elements with which the behaviour of the objects of a domain may be modelled, and knowledge about their properties and the ways in which they can be connected together. The authors of *IDM* contend that the behaviour of mechanical devices can be completely modelled with the aim of only five basic modelling elements. These elements are transformers, regulators, reservoirs, conduits and joints. By drawing on the physical knowledge base, the simulator builds models and investigates their behaviour.

Inference begins with a consultation with the user about the problem to be tackled. The information gathered is used to fill the slots of the frames in the frame system of the experiential knowledge base until a frame is

Advanced Students' Guide to Expert Systems

confirmed, which gives an entry point to the semantic network. The consultation will also gather a definition of the problem, from which a model will be constructed by the physical knowledge base. The simulator will then determine from the model whether a genuine problem exists. If there is a problem, the overall inference engine will direct the experiential knowledge engine to diagnose a solution and recommend a course of action. The experiential knowledge engine can start to do this from the point indicated by the confirmed frame. It may be able to find a course of action to solve the problem without help, or it may need to call on the physical knowledge engine for assistance, perhaps to obtain a more detailed understanding of the mechanism of the malfunction or to provide a detailed justification of its recommendation.

CLINAID

CLINAID is another medical expert system, in this case designed to meet the perception that clinicians need help with more than just the decisions on how to treat their patients. The diagnosis of a patient's illness will require a consultation, and this must be recorded. At the same time, information already held on the patient may be needed, for example, to help understand the progress of a disease suffered by the patient. Then, if a diagnosis can be made, it is likely to be only one of a number of factors affecting the decision on what treatment should be given. The patient's records need to be consulted to avoid the recommendation of an inappropriate treatment, such as a drug that will cause an allergic reaction. Clearly, the clinician will benefit from a system that can automatically update patient records and consult them at the appropriate times during the patient treatment.

CLINAID has been produced in response to this analysis of clinicians' needs. Its architecture consists, as shown in Figure 7.11, of:

- a *diagnostic unit*, which can question its user to collect the information it needs. While it lacks sufficient information to make a diagnosis, it attempts to collect further information, progressively narrowing its set of possible diagnoses. Eventually, it will produce a diagnosis or offer a range of possible diagnoses

- a *treatment recommendation unit*, which advises on the treatment that the patient should receive, taking into account not only the diagnosis generated by the diagnostic unit but also any relevant details of the patient held by the patient record unit

Some expert systems

```
                    ┌──────────────┐
                    │ Treatment    │
┌──────────┐        │ recommendation│
│Diagnostic│        │ unit         │────▶ User
User──▶│unit      │        └──────────────┘
    └──────────┘              ▲
         │  ▲                 │
         ▼  │                 │
        ┌──────────────┐
        │ Co-ordinator │
        │ unit         │
        └──────────────┘
              ▲
              ▼
        ┌──────────────┐
        │ Patient      │
        │ record       │
        │ unit         │
        └──────────────┘
```

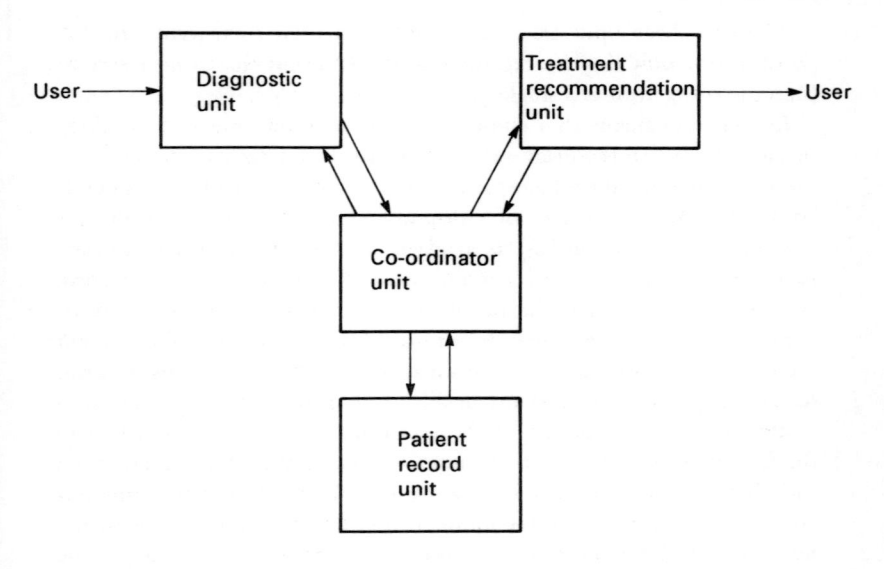

Figure 7.11 *The architecture of* CLINAID

- a *patient record unit*, which keeps details of patient's clinical records and allows that information to be updated, supplemented and retrieved as required. It is this capability that releases the clinician from the chore of having to write up the details of a consultation and guarantees the production of complete and reliable records of consultations. It also ensures that all the relevant information about a patient can be taken into account at the crucial times
- a *co-ordinator unit*, which allows the other units to co-operate by acting as a medium for information exchange. A diagnosis from the diagnostic unit, for example, is passed to the treatment recommendation unit via this unit. But this action indicates, among other things, that a consultation has taken place at the diagnostic unit. Thus, on receipt of a diagnosis, the co-ordinator unit can request the details of its last consultation from the diagnostic unit and pass them to the patient record unit. In ways such as this, the co-ordinator unit not only enables communication between units, but controls their interaction and ensures that the information necessary to the current activity of each unit is always provided.

Advanced Students' Guide to Expert Systems

The first three units are expert systems in their own right, and the co-ordinator unit may be regarded as an extra unit that is necessary to bind them together as a single system.

Inference begins with a consultation between the user and the diagnostic unit. When the diagnostic unit has made a diagnosis, it sends it to the co-ordinator unit which passes it on to the treatment recommendation unit. But the receipt of a diagnosis indicates to the co-ordinator unit that a consultation has taken place and that the treatment recommendation unit will need certain details from the patient's record. Accordingly, it requests the details of the consultation from the diagnostic unit and passes them to the patient record unit. The patient record unit consolidates the information it receives into its records, following which it can pass any details of the patient that are relevant to treatment recommendation to the co-ordinator unit for forwarding to the treatment recommendation unit. On receipt of both a diagnosis and the relevant information about the patient, the treatment recommendation unit can generate a recommendation and communicate it to the user. It will also send it to the co-ordinator unit to be passed to the patient record unit and entered in the records.

TK!Solver

TK!Solver is, to simplify somewhat, a program for solving equations. It can solve equations containing only one mention of a variable directly (that is, by a method equivalent to re-arranging the equation to make the one occurrence of the variable the subject of the equation) and equations that mention their variable more than once indirectly (that is, by an iterative procedure). It deals with sets of equations in a corresponding fashion. Equations can involve quantities expressed in different units, and can incorporate standard mathematical functions or user-defined functions. The user has only to enter the variables involved in the equations, their units and the equations themselves, and the program solves the equations and presents the results.

The general structure of *TK!Solver* is shown in Figure 7.12. A comparison with Figure 2.16 shows that the structure is that of an expert system. The user interface consists of a set of electronic 'sheets', with one for variables, one for units, one for equations and so on. Entries are made on the appropriate sheet. The entered information is added to the knowledge base. This already contains, among other things, rules for

Some expert systems

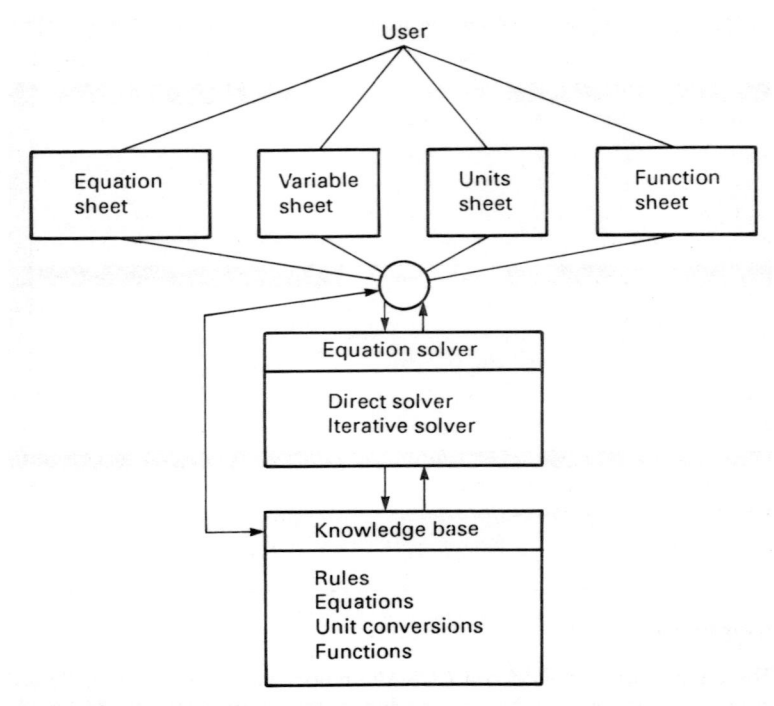

Figure 7.12 *The architecture of* TK!Solver

manipulating equations and for the selection of equation-solving method; unit conversion facilities; and mathematical functions. When all the necessary information has been entered on the sheets, the units are automatically adjusted, any functions evaluated, the equations solved, and the results returned to the appropriate sheet. Results appear as shown in Figure 7.13.

As a readily available microcomputer program, *TK!Solver* may not always be thought of as an expert system, although it certainly has the same form as one. The knowledge in its knowledge base does not all come from humans: its indirect solution method is essentially a generally applicable method and not a collection of expertise on equation-solving. But it is a rapid equation-solver and can out-perform expert human equation-solvers. In addition, its user interface and ease of use are prime examples of how simple it can be to use a complex program.

Advanced Students' Guide to Expert Systems

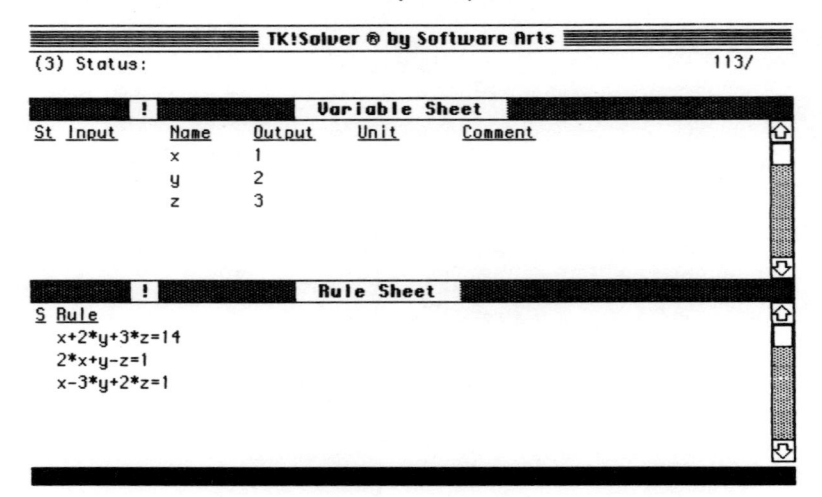

```
═══════════════ TK!Solver ® by Software Arts ═══════════════
(3) Status:                                              113/
┌─────────────────── Variable Sheet ───────────────────┐
St  Input     Name    Output    Unit    Comment
              x       1
              y       2
              z       3


┌─────────────────── Rule Sheet ───────────────────┐
S  Rule
   x+2*y+3*z=14
   2*x+y-z=1
   x-3*y+2*z=1
```

Figure 7.13 *A TK!Solver display*

Assignment 7

The architectures of *IDM* and *CLINAID* render these systems suitable for applications other than the ones for which they were originally designed. Compile a list of possible applications for each system. For each of the applications suggested for *IDM*, try to devise a set of basic modelling elements in terms of which the simulator can model all the domain activities. Explore the requirements imposed on the co-ordinator unit for each application suggested for *CLINAID*.

Recap

- descriptions of the architectures and modes of operation of three classic expert systems have been given to show how the commonly used schemes for representing knowledge, and the associated means of making inferences from that knowledge, have been implemented in practice. The systems are *MYCIN*, which is rule-based; *CASNET*, which makes use of semantic nets; and *PIP*, which uses frames.

Some expert systems

- three more recently developed systems are described to show exactly how the basic expert systems architecture has been elaborated in practice. The consequences of these innovative architectures for the modes of operation of the systems are also explored. The systems are *IDM*, which has two knowledge bases that deal with knowledge at different levels; *CLINAID*, with its distributed architecture; and *TK!Solver*, which has a novel user interface.

8: Expert systems and tutoring

Objectives

After reading this chapter, you should be able to:

- outline the history of the use of computers for educational purposes
- appreciate that a knowledge base acquired for an expert system is also a potential source for the teaching of that expertise
- recognize that an expert system with good explanatory facilities has a certain educational value
- explain why a system for teaching the contents of a knowledge base also needs expertise in tutoring
- derive descriptions of the various component parts of an expert tutoring system
- describe methods by which a model of student performance may be obtained
- design the architecture of an expert tutoring system, given the component parts of the system and a method of assessing student performance.

Scenario

The Head of Research spotted Dr Newman and the Senior Scientist dining together in the hospital refectory and went over to join them.

'Your brain child is doing very well in its trials, Dr Newman.'
'I don't think that's very funny!'
'Sorry. Just a turn of phrase. But I thought you'd like to know.'
Turning to the Senior Scientist, he went on:

'The thought I have now is that we have to hand this knowledge about diagnosing pulmonary infections, which seems to be the genuine article. Surely we ought to be able to use it to train our medical students. I don't suppose you know anyone who can help us with that, do you?'

Expert systems and tutoring

An expert system has, in its knowledge base, a compendium of knowledge and, in its inference engine, a means of using that knowledge to achieve certain goals. *MYCIN*'s knowledge base, for example, contains rules relating to the collection of the necessary data about a patient and rules for the diagnosis of infectious diseases: its inference engine uses the rules from the knowledge base to make diagnoses and then to produce treatment recommendations. This knowledge and the way it is used represent exactly the skills that a potential clinician needs to acquire. The thought naturally arises that it ought to be possible to use *MYCIN* to train clinicians just as it ought to be possible to use other expert systems to help educate the next generation of experts in their fields of expertise.

A number of systems have been developed in the course of trying to harness expert systems as tutors. Some attempts have met with a measure of success: some have revealed that the resulting systems inevitably have shortcomings, but have also indicated other ways to proceed. One reason that an expert system cannot necessarily be re-shaped as a tutoring system is that while the level of explanation it produces may be suitable to a user experienced in its domain, its explanations may not be suitable for novices. Another, more basic, reason is that a system designed for one purpose is unlikely to fulfil another.

The use of computers for instruction and tutoring has a comparatively lengthy history. The earlier attempts were essentially of two kinds:

- programmed learning and drills. Programmed learning consists, in essence, of the presentation of a screen of information, followed by a set of questions designed to test the user's understanding of the material. Correct responses from the student lead to the next screen presenting new material, while incorrect responses cause either the repetition of the original information or a new display presenting the same material in a different way. This form of learning differs very little from the use of a programmed-learning text book. Drill programs test the user's grasp of a particular topic by posing a set of questions and problems. The designer of the drill attempts to anticipate the more likely responses to each question and to associate with each some appropriate guidance towards the correct answer. Correct answers are re-inforced, while the anticipated incorrect answers produce assistance, and a catch-all category for responses that are both incorrect and un-anticipated offers another attempt at answering the question. Well-designed drills can be an effective way of learning and of revising a narrow topic.

Advanced Students' Guide to Expert Systems

- exploring an environment. The computer can support quite rich environments, which are sometimes known as *microworlds*, and can allow their exploration. By providing a worthwhile environment and providing for its exploration, the computer can provide a basis for learning by experiment, by investigation, or by trial and error.

One difference between these two approaches to using the computer as a learning aid is that the provision of an environment for exploration supports only learning by discovery which, although undirected, is an entirely natural mode of learning, while drill programs implement a specific theory of learning, even though it is one that has fallen into disrepute. Both approaches can be adopted to harness expert systems so that they can be used for learning. An expert system can be used, perhaps with minor enhancements, for browsing. A tutoring module can be placed between the user and the expert system to direct its interaction with the user by implementing a specific learning theory. The following sections consider the possibilities of these two approaches.

Question 1

Some question-and-answer style drill programs repeatedly present questions and offer a number of possible answers from which one must be chosen. The set of answers often consists of the correct answer, several near-misses and a 'distractor'. For example, the question:'What is the capital of France?' might be accompanied by the choice: 'Paris, Bonn, Madrid, Amsterdam, Plaster'. The first, of course, is the correct answer: the last is the distractor. Give a definition of a distractor, and explain its purpose.

Question 2

Explain the ubiquitous use of the near-miss.

Expert systems as browsers

An expert system can of course be utilized by a user who is a novice to its domain quite as well as by a user experienced in the domain. The novice user may be able to learn something of the domain expertise that is embedded in the system simply by using the system and so, in the process, exploring the domain. It will not be sufficient, though, for the novice

Expert systems and tutoring

clinician to have access to a medical expert system and the records of a set of patients, and to observe the system in the course of diagnosing the patients' diseases. Access to some sort of explanatory facilities will be needed. Now, in general, a well-implemented expert system will possess some means of explanation, if only to give its regular users confidence in its results. Typically, it will be able to answer two kinds of queries:

- How? – To ask, when the system presents a recommendation or conclusion: 'How was that conclusion reached?'
- Why? – To ask, when the system requests an input: 'Why is this information required?'

In a system such as *MYCIN*, in which knowledge is represented by rules and inference takes place by rule-chaining, both types of question can be answered by reproducing a chain of rules. If the system has just presented the conclusion C, and the user asks: 'How (did you reach the conclusion C)?', the system can give an answer such as:

> The conclusion C was reached because:
> IF B THEN C,
> IF A THEN B, and
> A is true.

In somewhat less abstract form, this might read as:

> The diagnosis of disease c was reached because:
> If symptom b is confirmed then the patient has disease c
> If test a is positive then symptom b is confirmed
> Test a is positive.

On the other hand, if the system has just requested the laboratory test be carried out, and the user asks: 'Why (do you want this test carried out)?', the system can give its response by listing the chain that it is trying to complete, in this way:

The test is required to help reach the conclusion C because it will give A, and

> IF A THEN B
> IF B THEN C

Again, a less abstract version might be:

> The test is required to help in diagnosing disease c because it will determine if test a is positive, and

Advanced Students' Guide to Expert Systems

If test *a* is positive then symptom *b* is confirmed
If symptom *b* is confirmed then the patient has disease *c*.

This illustration should serve to demonstrate that expert systems can be used for browsing and that, as long as they give explanations of their actions, they can produce their knowledge and demonstrate the way they use it to the enquiring user. If it is possible to alter the details of the patient records, the user can even experiment with the system. The questions that have to be asked are: 'Are the explanations at all helpful to the user?' and 'Are they as helpful as they might be?'

It can be said at once that the explanations are not as helpful as they might be. The knowledge is expressed in terms of the 'tricks of the trade' and short-cuts of experts. To the extent that each item of knowledge is based on a thorough understanding of the domain and therefore distils a greater or lesser amount of knowledge and understanding, it may or may not be possible for the novice to appreciate its significance or to connect it with his own far lesser knowledge. When knowledge is represented by rules, the problem is compounded because no matter how much expertise is compiled into one item of knowledge, the representation is still exactly the same, with no clue to the degree to which the knowledge is distilled. For these reasons, the way in which a system presents its explanations is not as useful to a novice as it might be, and at the extreme may be of no use at all. (This is in no way a criticism of expert systems because in assessing them as learning systems, we are looking at them as something they were not intended to be.)

It is certainly possible to find ways of lessening the effects of these shortcomings. One way is to add a second knowledge base to the system in the way adopted by *IDM*, complementing the conventional knowledge base, *IDM*'s experiential knowledge base, with a second, physical, knowledge base and simulator. This would provide a means of expressing explanations in terms of basic elements that would be familiar to the novice user. Explanations could be given for lines of reasoning, or the underlying basis of each item of knowledge involved in a line of reasoning could be explained. In either case, the conventional knowledge base could provide an entry point for the physical knowledge base and its simulator could begin to generate explanations at a level more suited to the novice user.

A second way to improve the effectiveness of the explanation facility would be to tag each item of knowledge with a more detailed explanation or justification expressed in terms that the novice user should com-

Expert systems and tutoring

prehend. This could be implemented in a rule-based system by extending the form of the rules to:

IF condition THEN action BECAUSE explanation

A more concrete instance might be:

IF test *a* is positive
   THEN symptom *b* is confirmed
   BECAUSE a positive result from test *a* indicates the presence of bacillus *x* which causes the patient to exhibit symptom *b* by its action on the nervous system

Activity

Amend the rules in the rule-base of Figure 6.1 by adding a BECAUSE tag to each rule so that clear explanations can be given. Check that the tags do give clear explanations by setting the system a typical task and then generating the response to a 'How?' query. See if the BECAUSE tags can be written in such a way that good explanations can be given by printing only the tag, and not the entire rule, for each rule in the chain.

Activity

Describe how explanations may be generated by systems using semantic nets for knowledge representation, and by systems that use frames.

Tutorial systems

An expert system can be upgraded to an intelligent tutoring system with the addition of the following modules:

- a *tutoring module*, to initiate the dialogue between the system and the user and to manage the dialogue
- a *student model module*, to maintain a model of the state of the user's knowledge so that the activities of the system can be geared to meet the individual needs of the user.

Advanced Students' Guide to Expert Systems

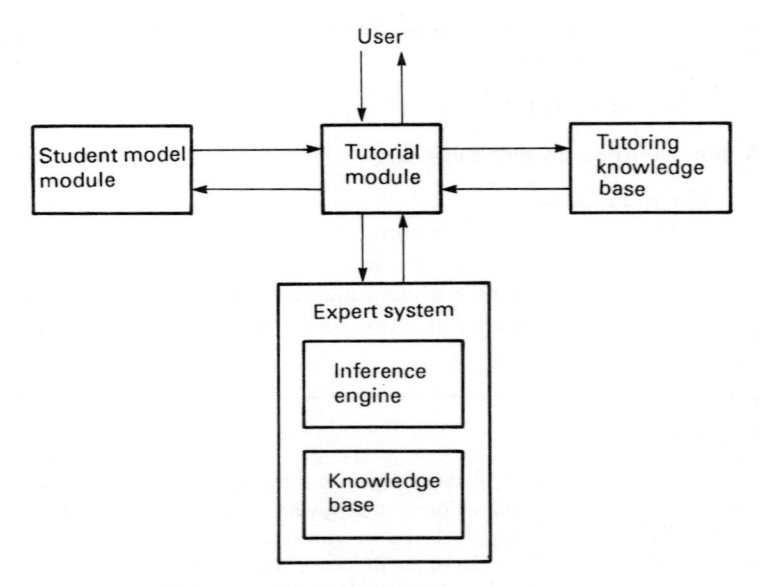

Figure 8.1 *Architecture of a tutorial system*

The general architecture for such a tutoring system is shown in Figure 8.1. A typical mode of operation is for the tutoring module to set a problem and to engage the expert system to solve it. Once the problem has been solved, the tutoring module can open the dialogue with the user, and set the problem. The tutoring module can then monitor the user's attempt at solving the problem and respond to any specific requests for help or information within the context of the learning theory governing its implementation. The dialogue provides information that can be incorporated in the student model regarding any aspect of the user's learning, ranging from his preferred mode of interaction with the computer to compiling a record of the knowledge that he has successfully learnt. The reasons for any incorrect actions on the part of the user must be diagnosed by the system so that it can guide the dialogue with the user in a way that will direct him to the knowledge that he needs to acquire.

There is scope for a considerable amount of variation within this general scheme for the operation of the system, as will be made clear by a consideration of the different ways that the tutoring and student model modules can fulfil their requirements.

The tutoring module should have access to knowledge of its own –

Expert systems and tutoring

knowledge of how to tutor – and in this sense, it is itself an expert system. If the tutoring knowledge base is kept separate from the knowledge base containing the problem-solving expertise that is to be imparted, the tutoring module can be developed without any dependence on the application area in which it is to be used. The module must communicate with the student, select problems to be solved, monitor the student's performance, diagnose from the student's responses any deficiencies in his acquisition of knowledge, generate a dialogue to make good the deficiencies and respond to requests for assistance.

The module should have access to tutoring knowledge that provides a means of generating the dialogue that is to take place with the student. The form of the dialogue can be governed by the structure of the knowledge to be imparted. It is possible for this to happen when the knowledge to be imparted deals with the way that a process develops over the course of time as, for example, with the sequence of cause and effect in the progress of a disease process or in the monthly and yearly cycles of the tides. The order in which events take place provides a natural ordering for the corresponding discourse. Dialogues can also be directed according to a learning theory. If the thrust of the tutorial method is to encourage the student to improve solution methods that are partially correct, or nearly correct, the Socratic method can be employed. Essentially, this involves repeated attempts to direct the student towards the ideas needed to modify his not-yet-correct method by asking questions such as: 'Why did you do this?' and 'Why not consider that?' Given that the module can diagnose the error in a solution method, it can continue the dialogue by generating an appropriate question designed to direct the user towards the discovery of that error.

In general, a dialogue manager must be able to deal with the various situations that recur in a tutorial dialogue, such as introducing a new topic, recognizing when a student has mastered a topic, and concluding the discussion of a topic.

The student model module is required to keep a record of the student's grasp of the material. This can be done in at least two ways. One is to make a copy of the knowledge that the student is to acquire, organize it into topics, and mark the topics that the student has mastered. By this means, the student's knowledge is described as a subset of the expert knowledge available to the system. A second way is to model the student's knowledge as a deviation from that of the expert. If the student's responses can be explained in terms of topics and basic procedures for making use of that knowledge, and the explanation shows some difference from any correct method, the deviation can then be seen as the source of error in the student's approach.

These two approaches imply their own ways of diagnosing the source of the student's errors. The first suggests that the student model be overlaid with the expert knowledge to reveal any relevant areas in which the student is lacking knowledge. The remedy is to present the missing knowledge. The second determines the source of error directly as a deviation. The lack of soundness in the approach can be pointed out and guidance as to a correct alternative can be introduced.

Question 3

Why is it a good idea to have a theory of learning on which to base the activity of the dialogue manager? Where are such theories drawn from?

Question 4

Why must a student model be incorporated in a tutoring system if it is to improve on the effectiveness of drill-type programs?

Alternative architectures

The two different approaches to creating a model of the student's knowledge lead to variations of the architecture of Figure 8.1. When the model records *what* the student knows, the student's knowledge can be assessed by overlaying it and the expert's knowledge to reveal any gaps. When the model is concerned with *how* the student proceeds to solve a problem, any incorrect procedures can be treated as procedures containing a 'bug' that needs to be corrected. The following sections consider the implications of these methods of assessing the student's knowledge on system architecture.

An architecture for overlaying

A student model suitable for assessment using the overlay technique needs to be able to recognize the topics present in the knowledge base, and to evaluate the student's mastery of each topic. The model can be maintained by the dialogue manager in the tutorial module. By first solving

Expert systems and tutoring

each problem that it presents to the user, the tutorial module can determine both the solution to the problem and the knowledge needed to solve the problem. Comparing the student's solution with the correct solution will show when the student has gone wrong. Overlaying the student's knowledge and the knowledge needed to solve the problem will reveal any gaps in the student's knowledge, and allow the dialogue to proceed in a way that will help the student. Figure 8.2 illustrates an architecture suitable for a system that will operate in this way.

One system that operates broadly in this way is *GUIDON*, a tutoring system for teaching the knowledge on diagnostic problem-solving contained in *MYCIN*. *GUIDON*'s student model records the degree to which the student has mastered each *MYCIN* rule in general, and the degree to which he is capable of applying it in solving the current prob-

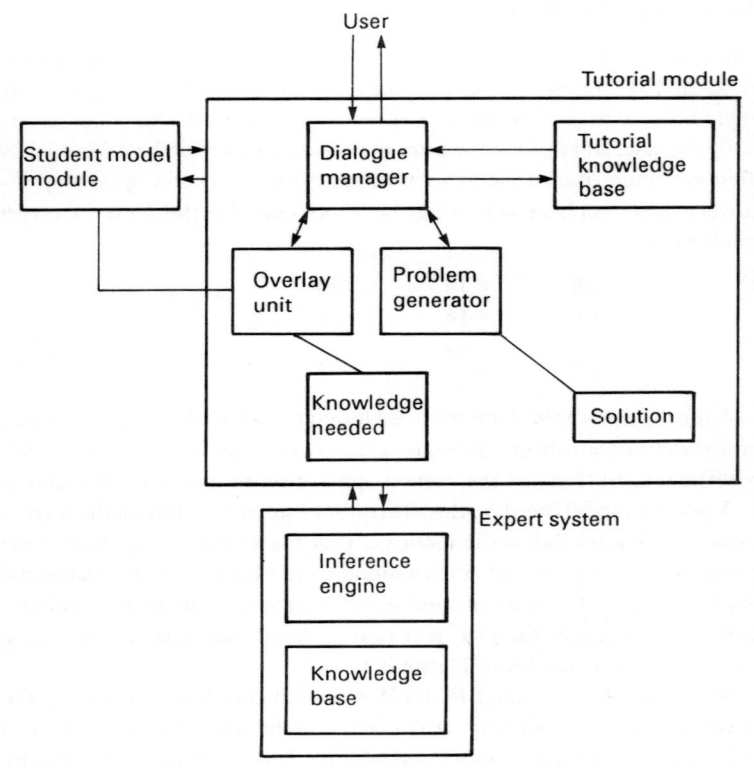

Figure 8.2 *Architecture for a tutorial system with overlaying*

Advanced Students' Guide to Expert Systems

lem. *GUIDON* begins by generating a problem and setting *MYCIN* to solve it. It then presents the problem to the student, but only after using the information that is known about the patient and the rules that can be applied to it to construct, by forward chaining, all the paths of reasoning that are valid in the circumstances. This allows the student's partial solutions to be judged by seeing if they correspond with one of the forward chains, while requests for information can be judged by whether they allow a chain to develop further towards the correct solution. An incorrect partial solution triggers an overlay of the student model so that any of *MYCIN*'s rules that the student needs but has not mastered can be detected. They can then be presented to the student by the tutorial module.

An architecture for bug detection

One response of teachers to children who cannot do arithmetic is that the children have mastered the necessary procedures but cannot correctly apply them with any consistency. It has been found that this is not necessarily the case, and that the mistakes the children make can be explained by their consistent use of incorrect procedures. Consider the following incorrect sums, each of which has been obtained by the same incorrect procedure:

```
   19         18         29
  + 8        +18        +21
  ---        ---        ---
   18         18         14
```

A mechanism of this kind has been found to explain faulty performance in a variety of situations. This gives rise to the idea of explaining faulty performance in terms of the correct application of incorrect procedures.

A student model based on this idea must be geared to finding the bugs in a student's knowledge as the incorrect procedures that are applied in the course of solving problems. Such a module must have access to a catalogue of procedures and a means of combining them to see if there is a combination that reproduces the incorrect results. An architecture incorporating such a module is shown in Figure 8.3.

A tutoring system called *BUGGY* intended precisely to diagnose the causes of students' arithmetic errors, and thereby to train teachers to help their students, operates on these broad lines. It has, in common with any system that adopts a similar approach, a greater capability than overlay

Expert systems and tutoring

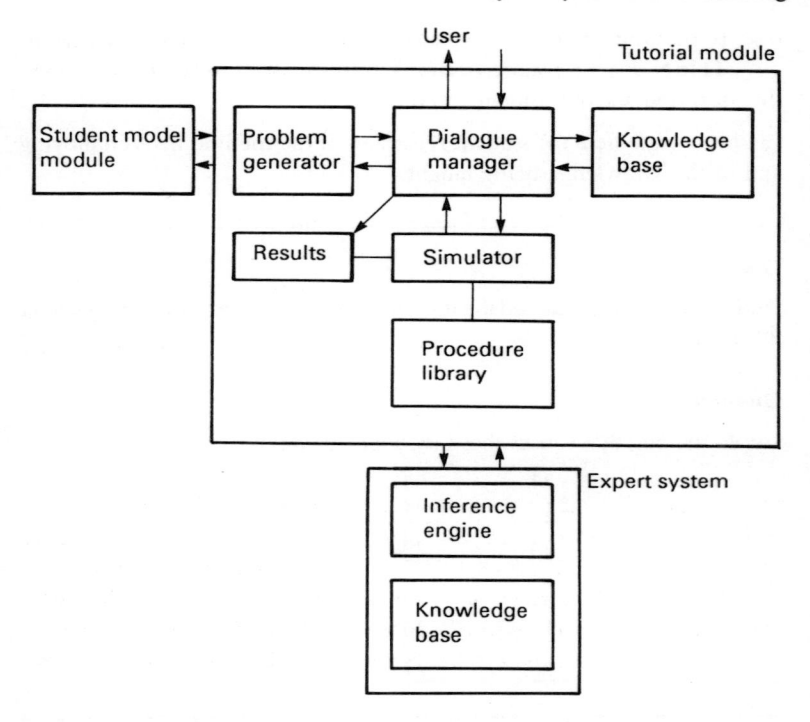

Figure 8.3 *Architecture for a tutorial system with bug detection*

systems in that it can permit the student to adopt not only the problem-solving methods of one expert but any correct method.

Other systems can accommodate different approaches to solving a problem by ensuring that the method adopted does not contain errors that can be classified into general types such as factual errors, reasoning errors, overgeneralization, and so on. Generalization is the process of moving from specific examples to a general explanation that covers the examples, perhaps in the sense that it could generate them. Overgeneralization is taking the process too far so that factors that are not relevant are included in the explanation. Thus, a series of pictures of houses might lead to the general explanation that 'an object is a house if it has windows, doors and a roof'. An overgeneralization would be: 'an object is a house if it has windows, doors, a roof and the picture was taken on a Wednesday'.

A tutorial system that can recognize an error of this kind and possesses in its knowledge base the rule:

Advanced Students' Guide to Expert Systems

IF the student gives an explanation containing an unnecessary factor
THEN select a counter-example to show that the factor is unnecessary and ask the student to consider it

can proceed to help the student regardless of the method he is employing and of the knowledge being taught.

Question 5
Find the bug that has caused the incorrect answers to the three sums given in this chapter.

Question 6
Locate the bug that causes these incorrect answers:

(i)
```
  31       55       27
 -17      -36       -9
  24       29       28
```

(ii)
```
  31       55       27
 -17      -36       -9
  26       21       22
```

Assignment 8
1 Criticize the overlay and bug techniques for assessing student performance. Can you devise an improved technique. If you can, could it be implemented?
2 Knowledge can be regarded as being built on levels. Concepts learnt in early life form a first level. Subsequently, a second level, based on first-level concepts, is developed. Thinking can then draw on the higher-level concepts of the second level, and first-level concepts can be discarded. The process continues to evolve. When it has passed through several levels, the concepts of the lowest levels are well and truly buried.

   Relate this idea of levels of knowledge to the generation of appropriate explanations by contrasting the knowledge levels of student and expert. How does this help towards a means of generating explanations at a suitable level?

Expert systems and tutoring

Recap

- the use of computers for education is one of the oldest themes in computing. Traditional educational programs have included drills and provided 'microworlds' for exploration.
- a knowledge base acquired for an expert system is a source of expertise that is potentially available to be taught. An expert system itself, although of some value in this respect, is not an ideal vehicle for teaching because its explanations are not expressed at a level suitable for anyone but an expert. An expert system can, though, be harnessed to form a component part of an expert tutoring system.
- the explanatory facilities of expert systems can be improved in various ways to make them suitable vehicles for learning in an essentially unstructured way.
- a tutoring system specifically designed to encourage some form of structured learning needs a knowledge base of teaching expertise, a dialogue manager and a student model. Different strategies exist for assessing the student's grasp of the knowledge being presented by the system. The general system requirements together with the requirements of a specific assessment strategy combine to dictate an architecture for the resulting tutorial system.

Answers to questions

1 A distractor is a potential answer that may distract the student from the correct answer, but it is one that should never be given as a genuine attempt at the answer. The distractor may provide some relief from the general drudgery of a drill, but its real purpose is to discourage a random choice of answer.
2 A near-miss should differ from a target goal in only one respect, making it easy to provide guidance about how to move from the near-miss to the target .
3 A theory provides a basis for deciding how to construct and continue a dialogue in a consistent and coherent way at all times. Theories can be drawn from subjects such as educational psychology and child psychology.
4 A system can only respond to a student in an individual way, as opposed to some generalized and shared way, by matching its response to the needs of that individual. To do this, it must have appropriate knowledge of the current state of that individual.

5 The results were obtained by adding up all the individual digits of the summands.
6 (i) The 'borrowed' ten has not been paid back. (ii) The smaller number has been subtracted from the larger in each column.

9: Dealing with uncertainty

Objectives

After reading this chapter, you should be able to:
- appreciate that expert systems can deal with knowledge that is uncertain and incomplete
- list ways in which different expert systems have coped with uncertainty
- represent uncertain knowledge by using relations
- express sets of relations as tables and matrices
- manipulate matrix representations of uncertain knowledge in order to effect inference.

Scenario

First Knowledge Engineer: 'How do you deal with uncertainty?'
Second Knowledge Engineer: 'I'm not sure.'

Expert systems must be able to deal with uncertainty. In situations where observations produce definite results and there is no doubt about which procedures are needed to process those results, expert systems are usually not needed because conventional programs are adequate. The presence of uncertainty, in fact, is one of the factors indicating that an expert system may well be needed.

Medical diagnosis is a prime example of an area in which decisions must be made despite the fact that the information available about the patient is often uncertain and incomplete. It is clearly not an option to wait until full information is available if the patient may die in the meantime! Risk management and many other applications share with medical diagnosis the characteristic that decisions must often be made in difficult and confusing circumstances.

Advanced Students' Guide to Expert Systems

We have already met expert systems that are capable of dealing with uncertainty. *CASNET* manages it by attaching the value of a confidence factor to the link between an observation and a disease state. The value indicates in an individual case the degree of confidence that can be placed in the existence of the disease state when the observation has been made. When several such links point to the same state, *CASNET* simply selects the confidence factor of greatest magnitude and uses it to decide whether the state can be confirmed or denied, or must remain undetermined. Although the decision procedure works, it does discard potentially useful information, which suggests that it could be improved upon. *MYCIN* can also cope with uncertainty. Many of its rules incorporate certainty factors, as in:

> IF the site of the culture is the throat
> AND the identity of the organism is streptococcus
> THEN there is suggestive evidence (certainty factor 0.8) that the subtype of the organism is not group-D

When *MYCIN* has constructed a chain of rules, each of which may involve a certainty factor, it has a procedure for combining the certainty factors of the rules in the chain. This gives an overall value for the certainty factor to be associated with the chain and so with its conclusion. The procedure has been the subject of some criticism but, again, it does work in practice.

Since there are shortcomings to the ways in which both *CASNET* and *MYCIN* deal with uncertainty, we will not pursue them further. Instead, in the remainder of this chapter, we will describe a straightforward way of representing uncertain knowledge and of computing the overall uncertainty associated with a chain of inference. The method is that used by *CLINAID*. The next section explains the basic ideas, showing how knowledge with no associated uncertainty is managed. The following section generalizes the method to deal with uncertainty.

Activity

Find out how *MYCIN* deals with uncertainty.

Knowledge representation and inference when there is no uncertainty

Suppose that we are intending to design an expert system for diagnosing patients' illnesses. A doctor goes about this by observing the symptoms of each patient, then trying to diagnose the illness from those symptoms. An expert system could do worse than to adopt the same approach. To begin, we certainly have to be able to record the patients' symptoms. Then we have to find a way of representing the knowledge about how symptoms relate to illnesses.

Representation

A natural way of representing observations of patients' symptoms is with a series of statements in the form:

patient1 displays symptom2

That is, with one or more statements of the general form:

– displays –

where the first slot is to be filled with the identity of a patient and the second with the name of a symptom.

The accumulated knowledge on a set of five patients, named *patient1* to *patient5*, assuming that they were expected to have a certain set of illnesses so that the only symptoms of interest were *S1* to *S5*, might be:

patient1 displays S2
patient1 displays S3
patient2 displays S2
patient3 displays S1
patient3 displays S4
patient3 displays S5
patient4 displays S2
patient4 displays S4
patient5 displays S1
patient5 displays S5

Note that a patient can display several symptoms. The knowledge in this set of statements is summarized in Table 9.1. The table does not give as clear a presentation of the knowledge as it might. A better presentation is provided by a matrix in which each row is labelled with the name of a

Table 9.1 Summarized knowledge on a set of patients

Patient	Symptom
Patient1	S2, S3
Patient2	S2
Patient3	S1, S4, S5
Patient4	S1, S4
Patient5	S2, S5

patient, and each column with the name of a symptom. The entries in the matrix are either 1 or 0 according to whether the patient whose name labels the row of the entry does or does not display the symptom whose name labels the column of the entry. When presented in this way, the knowledge appears as in Table 9.2. Note that the knowledge about a patient can be obtained by reading along a row: the positions of the 1s correspond to the observed symptoms. Reading down a column gives information about a symptom, with the frequency of its occurrence given by the number of 1s in the column.

Table 9.2 Matrix representation of knowledge in Table 9.1

	S1	S2	S3	S4	S5
Patient1	0	1	1	0	0
Patient2	0	1	0	0	0
Patient3	1	0	0	1	1
Patient4	1	0	0	1	0
Patient5	0	1	0	0	1

At this point, we have found a way to represent knowledge about patients. What is needed next is a way of representing the knowledge about the illnesses that the patients might have. But it can be represented in exactly the same way with statements such as:

symptom1 is an indication of illness3

These are particular cases of the general form:

− is an indication of −

where the first slot is to be filled by a symptom and the second by an illness.

Let us assume that the set of symptoms, $S1$ to $S5$, is related to the illnesses $I1$ to $I5$ in the following way:

Dealing with uncertainty

S1 is an indication of I1
S1 is an indication of I3
S2 is an indication of I2
S2 is an indication of I4
S3 is an indication of I5
S4 is an indication of I1
S4 is an indication of I2
S5 is an indication of I3
S5 is an indication of I4

A tabular presentation of this data (Table 9.3) makes clear that the various illnesses have different numbers of symptoms. The matrix representation is shown, on the other hand, in Table 9.4.

Table 9.3 *Summarized presentation of illnesses and symptoms*

Illness	Symptom
I1	S1, S4
I2	S2, S4
I3	S1, S5
I4	S2, S5
I5	S3

Table 9.4 *Matrix representation of the knowledge in Table 9.3*

	I1	I2	I3	I4	I5
S1	1	0	1	0	0
S2	0	1	0	1	0
S3	0	0	0	0	1
S4	1	1	0	0	0
S5	0	0	1	1	0

With these means of representing each patient with the symptoms he presents, and the set of symptoms that indicates each expected illness, we next need a means of inference that will allow us to infer the illness suffered by each patient.

Question 1

How can the patient–symptom matrix given above be used for information retrieval? Give a precise instruction for retrieving and printing the symptoms of a specified patient.

Advanced Students' Guide to Expert Systems

Inference

It is clear, for example, that when patient P4 has symptoms S2 and S4, and the presence of the symptoms S2 and S4 indicates illness I2, we should conclude that patient P4 is suffering from illness I2. In general, if the symptoms offered by a patient are the same as the symptoms of an illness, then the patient may be diagnosed as suffering from that illness. In terms of the matrix representations, this means that if a row of the patient–symptom matrix, when read from left to right, is the same as a column of the symptom–illness matrix, when read from top to bottom, then it can be concluded that the patient labelling the row has the illness labelling the column.

The procedure for inferring the illnesses suffered by patients can be carried out automatically by first writing the patient–symptom matrix and the symptom–illness matrix beside each other, thus:

```
0 1 1 0 0    1 0 1 0 0
0 1 0 0 0    0 1 0 1 0
1 0 0 1 1    0 0 0 0 1
1 0 0 1 0    1 1 0 0 0
0 1 0 0 1    0 0 1 1 0
```

Next, a third matrix is derived by comparing the rows of the first matrix with the columns of the second. Typically, the element in the second row and the third column of the new matrix is obtained by comparing the second row of the first matrix with the third column of the second matrix. If they are the same, the element is a 1; if they are different, the element is a 0. In this case, the new matrix is:

```
0 0 0 0 0
0 0 0 0 0
0 0 0 0 0
1 0 0 0 0
0 0 0 1 0
```

Finally, the matrix is interpreted by taking a 1 in row i and column j to mean that patient Pi is suffering from disease Ij. In this case, the diagnoses are that patient P4 has disease I1, and patient P5 has disease I4.

A means of automatically computing the patient–illness matrix of diagnoses can also be given. First, a notation is introduced in which we denote the patient–symptom matrix by P, and the element in row i and column j of this matrix by $p(i, j)$. Correspondingly, the symptom–illness matrix is denoted by S and its elements by $s(i, j)$; and the patient–illness matrix by D and its elements by $d(i, j)$.

Dealing with uncertainty

Now the elements of D can be computed from those of P and S by using the formula:

$$d(i, j) = \text{AND}_{(k=1..5)} \{ p(i, k) \text{ EQUIV } s(k, j) \}$$

where a set of values ANDed together give the value 0 unless all of them are 1. The operator EQUIV is computed from:

EQUIV	0	1
0	1	0
1	0	1

This can be illustrated as follows:

$$\begin{aligned}d(4, 1) &= \text{AND } \{p(4,1)\text{EQUIV } s(1,1), p(4,2) \text{ EQUIV } s(2,1) \ldots \\ &\qquad p(4,5)\text{EQUIV } s(5,1)\} \\ &= \text{AND } \{1 \text{ EQUIV } 1, 0 \text{ EQUIV } 0, 0 \text{ EQUIV } 0, 1 \text{ EQUIV} \\ &\qquad 1, 0 \text{ EQUIV } 0 \} \\ &= \text{AND } \{1, 1, 1, 1, 1 \} = 1\end{aligned}$$

This illustrates the way that exact diagnoses can be made. There are, however, ways of making inferences helpful to diagnosis even when exact diagnosis is not possible. One such inference would be to find whether all the symptoms of a patient were those of one particular illness, even if the patient does not show all the symptoms of that illness. Being able to detect the situation in which a patient has, say, two of the three symptoms of a particular disease, suggests not only that the patient might well have that disease but also that the doctor ought to look for the missing symptom.

This form of inference can be made by comparing the row for a patient and the column for an illness and drawing the conclusion unless a 1 from the row lines up with a 0 from the column. In these circumstances, the matrix inferred from the matrices P and S given above would be:

$$\begin{matrix} 0 & 0 & 0 & 0 & 0 \\ 0 & 1 & 0 & 1 & 0 \\ 0 & 0 & 0 & 0 & 0 \\ 1 & 0 & 0 & 0 & 0 \\ 0 & 0 & 0 & 1 & 0 \end{matrix}$$

The formula for computing the diagnosis matrix requires only a slight modification to the earlier one. It is:

$$d(i, j) = \text{AND}_{(k=1..5)} \{ p(i, k) \text{ IMP } s(k, j) \}$$

where the operator IMP is computed from:

IMP	0	1
0	1	1
1	0	1

Question 2

Adapt the procedure just given so that rather than finding whether a patient's symptoms form a subset of the symptoms of a disease, it determines whether the symptoms of the disease form a subset of the patient's symptoms. When this is the case, it means that the patient has all the symptoms of the disease, and possibly others. Which of the two situations would you consider most helpful to diagnosis?

Question 3

Say whether each of the following is true:

(i) If $A = B$ and $B = C$ then $A = C$

(ii) If A is nearly equal to B and B is nearly equal to C then A is nearly equal to C

(iii) If X is the same as Y and Y is the same as Z then X is the same as Z

(iv) If X is nearly the same as Y and Y is nearly the same as Z then X is nearly the same as Z.

Question 4

Explain the difference between the statements from Question 3 that are true and the others.

Representation and inference with uncertainty

The circumstances of the previous section are not realistic in so far as they suppose complete certainty in the observation of symptoms and in the connection between symptoms and illnesses. This section describes ways

Dealing with uncertainty

of representing and making inferences from knowledge that is not certain. The methods are direct generalizations of those of the previous section.

Representation

Let us repeat the exercise of the previous section, but with the premise that it is not always possible to be completely confident that a patient presents a particular symptom. In these circumstances, the knowledge about the relation between a patient and a symptom can be recorded by a statement with the form:

− displays − with degree of certainty −

where the first slot is to be filled with the name of a patient, the second with the name of a symptom and the third with the value of a factor indicating the extent to which the patient displays the symptom. A value of 0 indicates a complete lack of certainty that the patient displays the symptom, while a value of 1 indicates complete certainty that the patient displays the symptom. In a particular case a set of observations might be recorded by:

    patient1 displays S2 with degree of certainty 0.7
    patient1 displays S3 with degree of certainty 0.8
    patient2 displays S2 with degree of certainty 0.5
    patient3 displays S1 with degree of certainty 0.6
    patient3 displays S4 with degree of certainty 0.5
    patient3 displays S5 with degree of certainty 0.8
    patient4 displays S2 with degree of certainty 0.7
    patient4 displays S4 with degree of certainty 0.3
    patient5 displays S1 with degree of certainty 0.1
    patient5 displays S5 with degree of certainty 0.6

These observations can be presented in matrix form, exactly as before, except that the values of the elements in the matrix are the degrees of certainty. The matrix, P, is given in Table 9.5.

Exactly the same considerations affect the relation between symptoms and illnesses in that there is seldom complete certainty that a symptom indicates a particular disease. To cope with this, relations between symptoms and illnesses can be expressed in the form:

− is an indication of − with degree of certainty −

Advanced Students' Guide to Expert Systems

Table 9.5 Matrix, P, of patients and symptoms, recording degrees of certainty

	S1	S2	S3	S4	S5
Patient 1	0	0.7	0.8	0	0
Patient 2	0	0.5	0	0	0
Patient 3	0.6	0	0	0.5	0.8
Patient 4	0.7	0	0	0.3	0
Patient 5	0	0.1	0	0	0.6

where the first slot is for the name of a symptom, the second for the name of an illness and the third, as before, for the value of a degree of certainty. The relevant medical knowledge might then consist of a set of statements such as:

S1 is an indication of I1 with degree of certainty 0.6
S1 is an indication of I3 with degree of certainty 0.6
S2 is an indication of I2 with degree of certainty 0.8
S2 is an indication of I4 with degree of certainty 0.8
S3 is an indication of I5 with degree of certainty 0.5
S4 is an indication of I1 with degree of certainty 0.9
S4 is an indication of I2 with degree of certainty 0.7
S5 is an indication of I3 with degree of certainty 0.5
S5 is an indication of I4 with degree of certainty 0.4

As before, these statements can be placed in matrix form to give a matrix S, shown in Table 9.6. The inclusion of certainty factors has allowed us to generalize our method of knowledge representation to cope with uncertainty.

Table 9.6 Matrix, S, of symptoms and illnesses, recording degrees of certainty

	I1	I2	I3	I4	I5
S1	0.6	0	0.6	0	0
S2	0	0.8	0	0.8	0
S3	0	0	0	0	0.5
S4	0.9	0.7	0	0	0
S5	0	0	0.5	0.4	0

Dealing with uncertainty

Inference

We would expect that inference can be carried out by somehow combining the matrices P and S to obtain a diagnosis matrix D. The elements of D will be certainty factors indicating the degree of certainty with which it can be concluded that a patient is suffering from an illness.

The degree to which a patient's symptoms form a subset of the symptoms of a disease can be computed as follows. First, write the matrices P and S beside each other, thus:

0	0.7	0.8	0	0	0.6	0	0.6	0	0
0	0.5	0	0	0	0	0.8	0	0.8	0
0.6	0	0	0.5	0.8	0	0	0	0	0.5
0.7	0	0	0.3	0	0.9	0.7	0	0	0
0	0.1	0	0	0.6	0	0	0.5	0.4	0

Next, combine the matrices to get the diagnosis matrix, D, by using the formula:

$$d(i, j) = \frac{1}{5} \sum_{k=1}^{5} \{ p(i, k) \text{ IMP } s(k, j) \}$$

where the operator IMP is defined by:

$$a \text{ IMP } b = \text{minimum } (1, 1 - a + b)$$

This can be illustrated as follows:

$$d(3,3) = \frac{1}{5} \{ p(3,1) \text{ IMP } s(1,3) + p(3,2) \text{ IMP } s(2,3) + \ldots + p(3,5) \text{IMP } s(5,3) \}$$

$$= \frac{1}{5} \{0.6 \text{ IMP } 0.6 + 0 \text{ IMP } 0 + 0 \text{ IMP } 0 + 0.5 \text{ IMP } 0 + 0.8 \text{ IMP } 0.5\}$$

$$= \frac{1}{5} \{ \min(1, 1) + \min(1, 1) + \min(1, 1) + \min(1, 0.5) + \min(1, 0.7) \}$$

$$= \frac{1}{5} \{1 + 1 + 1 + 0.5 + 0.7\}$$

$$= 4.2/5 = 0.84$$

Advanced Students' Guide to Expert Systems

This means that the degree to which the symptoms of Patient 3 form a subset of the symptoms of the illness $I3$ is 0.84. The complete form of the matrix, D, is:

$$\begin{matrix} 0.7 & 0.84 & 0.7 & 0.84 & 0.8 \\ 0.9 & 1 & 0.9 & 1 & 0.9 \\ 0.84 & 0.72 & 0.84 & 0.7 & 0.62 \\ 0.98 & 0.86 & 0.92 & 0.8 & 0.8 \\ 0.86 & 0.88 & 0.96 & 0.96 & 0.86 \end{matrix}$$

There are other accepted ways to write the formula for computing D and to generalize the operator IMP. These ways will have different meanings associated with them: each will match an application according to the appropriateness of its particular meaning.

Activity

Criticize the operator IMP as defined above in terms of the results it produces. Determine whether either of these alternative definitions produces better results:

- a IMP b = 1 − a + ab
- a IMP b = maximum(1 − a, b).

Assignment 9

Devise a document retrieval system based on the following pair of relations. The first specifies the degree of a customer's interest in a particular topic, thus:

__ is interested in __ with degree of interest __

The slots are to be filled by a customer's name, the name of a topic and a degree of interest, assessed on a scale from 0 to 1. The second relation gives the extent to which a topic is covered by a document. Its form is:

__ is covered by __ with degree __

The slots are to be filled by the name of a topic, the name of a document and the degree, assessed on a scale from 0 to 1, to which the topic is treated by the document.

Dealing with uncertainty

Write down, in the style presented in this chapter, a set of relations giving the requirements of 6 customers, and a second set describing the topics covered by a set of 6 documents. Express each set in matrix form. Then carry out the inference procedure to determine the degree to which the documents meet the customers' requirements. Determine which document is best suited to each customer. Try the other versions of the IMP operator to see if they produce the same recommendations.

Recap

- expert systems can deal with knowledge that is uncertain and incomplete. Indeed, the need for systems that can cope in such circumstances is part of the reason for the existence of expert systems. Conventional programs can usually deal with situations in which there is no uncertainty. There is, however, no single accepted way of handling uncertainty, and different approaches have been adopted by different systems
- a method based on the idea of a relation is presented for representing knowledge that has a degree of uncertainty associated with it. A set of relations can be written in matrix form. Inference can then be achieved by combining two such matrices. It is shown that different types of inference can be achieved within this framework and that, according to their interpretations, they will be more or less appropriate in given circumstances. Also, different definitions can be adopted for the operators involved in the evaluations of the inference process, and these will correspond more or less closely to the reality of a specific situation.

Answers to questions

1 If patient is *Patient i* then {for k = 1 to 5; (if table(i, k) = 1 then write ('Patient *i* offers symptom', k) }
2 The adaptation requires IMP to be replaced by an operator named, say, RIMP, defined by:

RIMP	0	1
0	1	1
1	1	0

Advanced Students' Guide to Expert Systems

If a patient has only the symptoms of a particular disease, but not all of them, it could suggest that the remaining symptoms of that disease have not yet developed or have not been noted. When a patient has all the symptoms of a disease plus some others, it could suggest that the disease is present, and is accompanied by others. Thus, both types of inference are of value.

3 (i) True (ii) Not necessarily true (iii) True (iv) Not necessarily true.
4 The relations in (i) and (iii) capture a precise, or certain, concept, and the precision can be propagated along a chain. The relations in (ii) and (iv) deal with an imprecise, or uncertain, relation. When the imprecision is propagated along a chain, it can accumulate and drift out of range.

10: Languages for writing expert systems

Objectives

After reading this chapter, you should be able to:

- explain why *Lisp* and *Prolog* are referred to as 'AI languages'
- describe the basic features of *Prolog*, and explain the approach to writing programs in *Prolog*
- write simple programs in *Prolog*
- describe the basic features of *Lisp*, and explain the approach to writing programs in *Lisp*
- write simple programs in *Lisp*.

Scenario

In the software house, the programmer has been summoned to his project supervisor's office.

'I read your report on functional programming and languages for it and, much to my surprise, I rather enjoyed it.'

'Thank you.'

'I suppose that you're proposing to write this system in a functional language. Before you do that, I think you should consider the other AI languages. I would appreciate it if you could produce another report along the lines of this one dealing with the other languages.'

In previous chapters, a number of designs for expert systems have been described. While a design is essential, eventually an expert system must be supported by a computer. The step leading from an abstract design to an

Advanced Students' Guide to Expert Systems

implemented system running on a computer is to express the design in a programming language. The immediate question is that of which language to use.

In principle, any programming language can be used. After all, *CASNET* is written in *FORTRAN* and *MYCIN* in *Lisp*, and it is difficult to imagine two more different languages. Given a completely free choice of the language in which to implement an expert system, the essential factor affecting the choice is the extent to which the languages suit the requirements of the design. If recursion is to be used, then a language supporting it, such as Lisp, is preferable to one such as *FORTRAN* that does not. This is not to say that recursion is impossible in *FORTRAN*: merely that the programmer must create the facilities necessary to support it. Clearly, this makes the programmer's task harder than it would be if the capability were built into the language. Similarly, if back-tracking is required, it is built into *Prolog* but not into any other language.

Again, if a design is conceived in terms of functions, as illustrated in Chapter 4, a functional language such as *Lisp* will be suitable. If knowledge representation and inference are expressed by relations, as they are in Chapter 9, then a relational language like *Prolog* is appropriate.

Perhaps the most common languages currently used for the implementation of expert systems are *Lisp* and *Prolog*. They are among the languages loosely referred to as 'AI languages', so called because they contain features designed to handle problems of the kind that occur in AI. One characteristic shared by *Lisp* and *Prolog*, as a consequence of their respective features, is that they can be used to write programs that examine other programs, and even themselves. This capability is needed, for instance, if a program is to explain its conclusions, for it can only do so by examining its own mode of operation.

The ensuing sections are devoted to introductions to *Lisp* and *Prolog*.

Prolog

A *Prolog* program consists of a sequence of clauses. A clause is a logical statement drawn from a restricted repertoire and expressed in the style supported by *Prolog*. One type of clause is used to represent facts. Its form can be illustrated by using it to record as facts the lines present in Figure 10.1 as:

    line – between(a, b).
    line – between(b, c).

Languages for writing expert systems

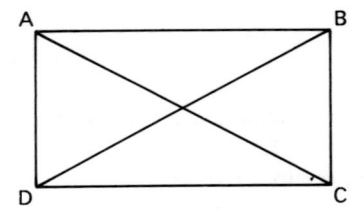

Figure 10.1 *A rectangle and its diagonals*

    line – between(c, d).
    line – between(d, a).
    line – between(a, c).
    line – between(b, d).

The use of *line – between* is intended to mean that there is a line between the first and second of the points named as its arguments. It does not matter to the computer what it means, though: the computer will simply manipulate it in a formal and consistent fashion. Note that lower-case letters have been used for the names of the points because they are instances of actual points. In *Prolog*, names beginning with capital letters indicate variables. Also, each clause must be terminated by a full stop.

This database of facts can now be queried. A query of the form:

    ?- line – between(a, c).

elicits the response *yes*, indicating that it is true. *Prolog* has determined this by trying to match it with each clause in turn until, at the fifth attempt, it finds a match. The query:

    ?- line – between(b, a).

draws the response *no* because there is no clause to match it. It may be objected that, in Figure 10.1, there is a line between points B and A. *Prolog* has not been told this, however. Its negative answer means that according to the facts it has been given, the answer to the query is *no*.

If there is a line from one point to a second, there clearly is a line from the second point to the first, even if it is just another way of looking at the same line. This deficiency in the way that the lines present in Figure 10.1 have been recorded in the database could be remedied by adding six clauses obtained by reversing the order of the points in the first six clauses to get:

159

Advanced Students' Guide to Expert Systems

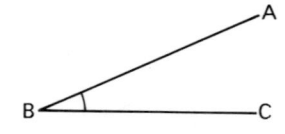

Figure 10.2 The angle ABC

>line – between(b, a).
>line – between(c, b).

and so on. We may also want to record the angles in the figure. This can be done by introducing the clause:

>angle(a, b, c).

to mean that there is an angle at point B in between the lines AB and BC, as shown in Figure 10.2. A series of clauses can then be written to record each of the angles in the figure. It is simpler, though, to use a second type of clause, known as a rule, because in this case the rule:

>angle(P, Q, R) :- line – between(P, Q), line – between(Q, R).

will suffice. The :- symbol is to be read as *if*; the comma as *and*; and P, Q and R indicate variables. The rule may be read as 'There is an angle PQR *if* there is a line between P and Q *and* there is a line between Q and R'. With the addition of this clause to the program, the response to:

>?- angle(a, b, c).

is *Yes*. *Prolog* has determined this by trying to find a matching fact, or a match on the left-hand side of a rule. In this case, none of the facts match, but the left-hand side of the new rule matches if P is set to *a*, Q to *b* and R to *c*. The left-hand side of the rule will be true if the condition on the right can be shown to be true. Because of the way the variables have been set for the matching, the condition becomes *line – between(a, b), line – between(b, c)*. The first of the clauses can be shown to be true by searching for a match from the beginning of the program, where the first clause duly matches. A match for the second is then sought, starting again at the beginning of the program, and found at the second attempt. A trace of this process can be written as:

>?- angle(a, b, c).
>   angle(P, Q, R)   P = a, Q = b, R = c

Languages for writing expert systems

    line − between(a, b)
      True
    line − between(b, c)
      True

At this point, we have met the three forms that a clause can assume. The most general is the rule, with a left-hand side and a right-hand side separated by the *if* symbol. The left-hand side is shown to be true by showing that the right-hand side is true. A fact is a rule with no right-hand side, that is, a left-hand side of a rule that is always true because it does not depend on any conditions. A query is a rule with no left-hand side: simply a condition that *Prolog* is to find true or false. In addition, a query, and the right-hand side of a rule, can consist of clauses ANDed together.

A query containing more than one clause appears as:

  ?− line(a, X), line(X, b).

It can be read as 'Find if there is a line between a and some intermediate point *and* a line between that same intermediate point and b'.

The following rule giving paths consisting of two lines also has more than one clause on its right-hand side:

  two − path(X, Y) :− line − between(X, Z), line − between(Z, Y).

It can be read as 'There is a path consisting of two lines between a first point and a second *if* there is a line between the first point and an intermediate point *and* a line between the intermediate point and the second point'. In effect, it is describing a way of solving the first problem by solving two simpler problems. *Prolog*'s response to the query:

  ?− two − path(a, c).

is *yes*. A trace of the solution is:

  ?− two − path(a, c)
    two − path(X, Y)   X = a, Y = c
      line − between(a, Z)   Z = b
        True
      line − between(b, c)
        True

Because of its ability to backtrack, *Prolog* finds more than one way of obtaining this solution, but the production of multiple solutions is better demonstrated with a simpler problem. Consider the query:

?- line – between(b, P).

Prolog's response to this is:

P = c;
P = d;
P = a;
No

This means that the query is satisfied in three different ways. Prolog finds them all: the final *no* indicates that there are no more solutions. The first solution is obtained by a match with the second clause; the second by a match with the sixth clause; and the third by a match with the seventh clause. The semicolon is usually typed by the user after one solution to trigger the search for the next one. The search resumes from where it left off. A trace of the process of finding the multiple solutions is:

```
?- line – between(b, P)
line – between(b, P)     P = c
    True
Output P = c
;
line – between(b, P)     P = d
    True
Output P = d
;
line – between(b, P)     P = a
    True
Output P = a
;
No
```

We now present two examples to show how problems can be solved by using facts to describe the basic situation and rules to provide some knowledge about it.

Example 1

Consider Figure 10.1 again. It displays a rectangle ABCD, with its diagonals. From a description of the rectangle and some basic knowledge about right-angled triangles, it is possible to prove that the diagonals of the rectangle are equal in length.

Languages for writing expert systems

We have already seen that the sides of the rectangle can be described by:

line – between(a, b).
line – between(b, c).
line – between(c, d).
line – between(d, a).
line – between(a, c).
line – between(b, d).
line – between(b, a).
line – between(c, b).
line – between(d, c).
line – between(a, d).
line – between(c, a).
line – between(d, b).

The angles can be described thus:

right – angle(a, d, c).
right – angle(b, c, d).
right – angle(c, d, a).
right – angle(a, b, c).

Some knowledge can now be added to the program. It states that if two right-angled triangles have bases and height of the same length, as shown in Figure 10.3, then their hypotenuses are also the same length. This is expressed by the rule:

equal – length(line – between(X, Z), line – between(P, R)) :-
  right – angle(X, Y, Z),
  right – angle(P, Q, R),
  equal – length(line – between(Y, X), line – between(Q, P)),
  equal – length(line – between(Y, Z), line – between(Q, R)).

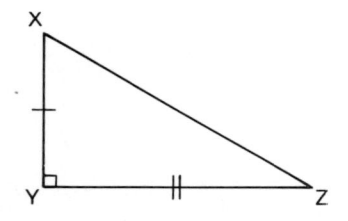

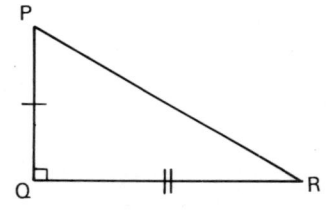

Figure 10.3 *Right-angled triangles of the same size and shape*

Advanced Students' Guide to Expert Systems

Finally, the fact that opposite sides are the same length along with some common-sense knowledge about equal lengths can be described by:

  equal − length(line − between(a, b), line − between(c, d)).
  equal − length(line − between(c, b), line − between(d, a)).
  equal − length(line − between(A, B), line − between(B, A)).
  equal − length(line − between(A, B), line − between(C, D)) :-
    equal − length(line − between(C, D), line − between(A, B)).

With this program, we can enquire whether the diagonals are equal by entering:

  ?- equal − length(line − between(a, c), line − between(b, d)).

The following trace shows how *Prolog* comes to give a positive response to this query.

  ?- equal − length(line − between(a, c), line − between(b, d)).
    equal − length(line − between(X, Z), line − between(P, R))
  X = a, Z = c, P = b, R = d
      right − angle(a, Y, c)   Y = d
        True
      right − angle(b, Q, d)   Q = c
        True
      equal − length(line − between(d, a), line − between(c, b))
      equal − length(line − between(A, B), line − between(C,D))
  A = d, B = a, C = c, D = b
        equal − length(line − between(c, b), line − between(d, a))
          True
      equal − length(line − between(d, c), line − between(c, d))
      equal − length(line − between(A, B), line − between(B, A))
  A = d, B = c
        True

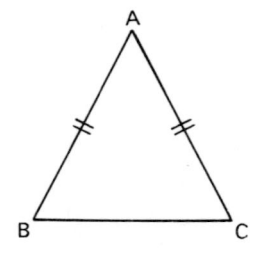

Figure 10.4 Given AB = BC, show that angle ABC = angle ACB

Languages for writing expert systems

Example 2

The aim of this problem is to solve the problem illustrated in Figure 10.4, by showing that when a triangle has two sides of equal length, the angles opposite those sides are also equal.

We can begin the program with a statement of the equality of the sides and some common-sense knowledge about equal lengths:

    equal − length(line − between(a, b), line − between(a, c)).
    equal − length(line − between(U, V), line − between(V, U)).
    equal − length(line − between(A, B), line − between(C, D)):-
        equal − length(line − between(D, C), line − between(B, A)).

Next, we add some general knowledge about triangles. This is that two triangles are congruent, that is, have the same size and shape, if their corresponding sides have the same lengths (see Figure 10.5):

    congruent(triangle(X, Y, Z), triangle(P, Q, R)):-
        equal − length(line − between(X, Y), line − between(P, Q)),
        equal − length(line − between(Y, Z), line − between(Q, R)),
        equal − length(line − between(Z, X), line − between(R, P)).

Finally, we add the general knowledge that if two triangles have the same size and shape then their corresponding angles must be equal:

    equal − angles(angle(A, B, C), angle(D, E, F)) :-
        congruent(triangle(A, B, C), triangle(D, E, F)).

Now we can put the query about the angles:

    ?- equal − angles(angle(a, b, c), angle(a, c, b)).

The reply is affirmative, and the trace is:

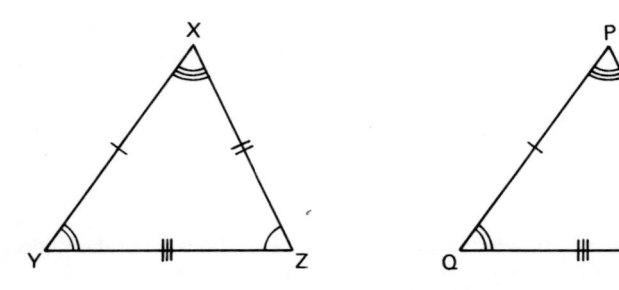

Figure 10.5 *The congruent triangles XYZ and PQR*

Advanced Students' Guide to Expert Systems

```
?- equal - angles(angle(a, b, c), angle(a, c, b)).
equal - angles(angle(A,B,C), angle(D,E,F))
A = a, B = b, C = c, D = a, E = c, F = b
   congruent(triangle(a, b, c), triangle(a, c, b))
   congruent(triangle(X,Y,Z), triangle(P,Q,R)
X = a, Y = b, Z = c, P = a, Q = c, R = b
       equal - length(line - between(a, b), line - between(a, c))
           True
       equal - length(line - between(b, c), line - between(c, b))
       equal - length(line - between(U, V), line - between(V, U))
U = b, V = c
           True
       equal - length(line - between(c, a), line - between(b, a)).
       equal - length(line - between(A, B), line - between(C, D))
A = c, B = a, C = b, D = a
       equal - length(line - between(a, b), line - between(a, c))
           True
```

Activity

Display the proofs in Examples 1 and 2 as resolution trees.

Question 1

Transform the way in which *Prolog* demonstrated the truth of the query in Example 1 to a proof expressed in purely geometric terms.

Question 2

Transform the way in which *Prolog* demonstrated the truth of the query in Example 2 to a proof expressed in purely geometric terms.

Languages for writing expert systems

Prolog's data structure is the list. A list is written either by enclosing its elements in square brackets and separating them by commas, so that the list of the three elements *a*, *b* and *c* is written as [*a*, *b*, *c*], or in the head and tail form described in Chapter 4 as [X | Y], where X is the head of the list and Y the tail. The list:

[a, b, c]

would match:

[X | Y]

with X = a and Y = [b, c]. The empty list, that is, the list of zero elements, is written [ ].

Lists can be manipulated in *Prolog* in the ways described in Chapter 4. A program to determine if an element is a member of a list is:

member(X, [X | Y]).
member(X, [Head | Y]) :- member(X, Y).

This may be interpreted as saying 'An element is a member of a list if it is the head of the list or if it is a member of the tail of the list'. The response to:

?- member(b, [a, b, c]).

is *Yes*, while a negative response will be given to:

?- member(d, [a, b]).

A program for appending two lists can be written as:

append(L, M, N).

It uses three arguments; the first and second are the lists to be appended and the third is the result of appending the first two. As an example:

append([a, c], [e, g], [a, c, e, g]).

is true. The program is based on the fact that if the first list, List 1, is empty then appending it to the second means that the third list will be the same as the second. Otherwise, the first list must have a head and so must have the form [*Head* | *List1*]. Appending this list to the second, List2, gives a list of the form [*Head* | *List3*] where List3 is obtained by appending List1 and List2. This gives the program:

append([ ], L, L).
append([X | List1], List2, [X | List3]):- append(List1, List2, List3).

167

Advanced Students' Guide to Expert Systems

The final example in this section illustrates how lists and list manipulation can be used in solving a problem.

Example 3

Suppose we have a network of points joined by lines as in Figure 10.1. The points could represent stations and the lines the links between them. If the links are described by a set of *line – between* clauses, it is possible to determine whether there is a route from one station to another with the program:

    route(X, X).
    route(X, Y):- line – between(X, Z), route(Z, Y).

This program does not give the route. In addition, it is possible for it to get stuck in a loop: with the configuration of Figure 10.1, for example, when trying to find a route from A to C, it is possible to get trapped in the loop connecting A, B and D. A program that finds the route from one station to another, keeps a record of the route and never visits the same point twice is:

    route(X, Y, [Y | Tail – stations]).
    route(X, Y, Stations) :-
    line – between(X, Z), not(member(Z, Stations)), route(Z, Y, [Z | Stations]).

The three arguments of *route* are for the starting station, the finishing station and a list of stations visited so far. The *not member* clause on the right of the rule ensures that no station that has previously been visited is included in the route again, so that no looping can occur. In the third clause, the station that has just been visited is added to the list of stations visited so far, simply by making it the head of the list. A typical request would take the form:

    ?- route(a, c, [a]).

Question 3

Write a *Prolog* program to find the length of a list.

Languages for writing expert systems

Question 4

Write a *Prolog* program to delete a given element from a list. (Hint: One way of writing it is so that *delete(b, [a, b, c], [a, c]) is true*.)

Lisp

Lisp is intended basically for processing lists. A list of items is represented by writing the names of the items separated by a space and enclosing them in brackets, thus:

   (A B C)

But a *Lisp* program is also written as a list: the first element of the list is a function and the rest of the elements are arguments for the function. A small program is:

   (PLUS 1 3)

where PLUS is one of the functions provided by *Lisp*, and the following numbers are its arguments. When this program is executed, it returns 4 as its result. To put this another way, 1 and 3 are regarded as the inputs to the function PLUS, and *Lisp* deals with the program by evaluating the output of the function.

In general, *Lisp* deals with a program by:

- evaluating the arguments. It does this by finding the values of all the items in the program list except the first
- applying the function to its evaluated arguments
- delivering the result.

Thus, *Lisp* is a functional language in the sense that its programs consist of functions and their arguments. *Lisp* provides some functions, such as PLUS, as the basic building blocks for programs, as well as the capability to define others. A complex program is a function in some way composed of, or built from, other functions.

We have shown in Chapter 4 how it is possible to describe activities with the use of functions. Once a procedure has been conceived in terms of a function, it only remains to express that function in the notation employed by *Lisp* to have a *Lisp* program. As the necessary background has been covered by Chapter 4, in the remainder of this section we present

Advanced Students' Guide to Expert Systems

some of *Lisp*'s own functions, show how to define new ones and give a few examples of programs in *Lisp*. It may prove useful to review Chapter 4 before proceeding with the remainder of this section.

A selection of the functions provided by *Lisp* follows.

Functions needed for technical reasons

- QUOTE, which simply delivers its argument, so that QUOTE(A) delivers A
- SET, which takes two arguments and sets the value of the first to the second. But care is needed here. The program (SET A 2) is dealt with by first evaluating its arguments. It may be that A has had a value assigned to it, although the value of 2 is 2. Thus the effect of the program will be to set whatever is obtained by evaluating A to 2. If we really want to set A to 2, we must write (SET QUOTE(A) 2)
- EQUAL, which takes two arguments and returns T (for true) if they are equal and F (for false) if they are not. The items compared can be numbers, but they can also be symbols or lists or anything else.

Arithmetic functions

- PLUS, which delivers the sum of its arguments, as we have seen
- TIMES, which delivers the product of its arguments, so that (TIMES 4 5) delivers 20. After (SET QUOTE(A) 2) and (SET QUOTE(B) 3), (TIMES A B) delivers 6 and (PLUS A B) delivers 5.

List handling functions

- CAR gives the head of a list, so that after (SET QUOTE(L) QUOTE((A B C))) to set L to the list (A B C), (CAR L) delivers A
- CDR gives the tail of a list, so that (CDR L) delivers the list (B C)
- CONS adds an element to the head of a list, so that (CONS QUOTE(H) L) delivers the list (H A B C)
- NULL to test for the empty list. NULL(()) is true, while NULL(L) is false when L has been set to any list other than the empty list.

Languages for writing expert systems

Functions allowing conditional actions

- COND. This allows conditional actions to be expressed in a way that corresponds exactly to the structure:
  if condition1 then action1 else
     if condition2 then action2 else
        if condition3 then action3 else
           ...
  It takes the form:
  (COND   (condition1   action1)
          (condition2   action2)
          ...
          (conditionm   actionm))

It is evaluated by testing successively condition1, condition2 and so on until a condition is found to be true. The action corresponding to this condition is then carried out.

Function allowing definition of new functions

- DEFINE. The function for defining new functions takes two arguments. The first is a list whose head is the name of the new function: the tail lists the arguments of the new function. The second is the description of the new function. An example may make this clearer. A function named ADDONE that adds one to its argument can be defined by (DEFINE (ADDONE X) (PLUS X 1)). After the new function has been defined, it can be used in the same way as any other, and (ADDONE 5) will give a result of 6.

A few of the functions introduced in Chapter 4 can now be written in *Lisp*. The function that gives the length of a list is:

(DEFINE   (LENGTH L)
   (COND((NULL L)   0)
        (T   (PLUS 1 (LENGTH (CDR L))))   ))

Here T stands for *true*, and is used to provide a condition that is always true. Its use ensures that the behaviour of COND corresponds to that of the if-then-else in the definition of *length* in Chapter 4.

The function for deciding if an element is a member of a list can be written as:

(DEFINE   (MEMBER X L)
   (COND((NULL L)   F)

171

Advanced Students' Guide to Expert Systems

```
((EQUAL X (CAR L))    T)
(T       (MEMBER X (CDR L)))    ))
```

We will end this introduction to *Lisp* with an example of a function for manipulating other functions. The function is called MAP, and it takes two arguments. The first is a function, the second a list. MAP applies the function to each element of the list in turn to produce a corresponding list as its output. To illustrate,

(MAP   ADDONE   QUOTE(2   4   6))

gives the list (3   5   7).

Question 5

Write a *Lisp* program that accepts two lists and delivers a single list consisting of the first list appended to the second.

Question 6

Write a *Lisp* program for the higher-order function MAP.

Assignment 10

Write a *Prolog* program for the knowledge base and inference engine of a miniature expert system based on the design given in Chapter 9 for a diagnostic system.

Recap

- as a computer-based artifact, an expert system must eventually be expressed as a computer program. The program must be written in a programming language, and the so-called 'AI languages', which include *Lisp* and *Prolog*, are prime candidates because they possess facilities specifically intended to meet the requirements of applications of this kind

Languages for writing expert systems

- *Prolog* and *Lisp* are described, along with the approaches that need to be taken when writing programs in these languages. A *Prolog* program consists of a sequence of clauses: the basic type of clause is simply a relation. A *Lisp* program is a function: it can combine other functions which, in turn, can be either the basic functions supplied by Lisp or functions previously defined by the programmer. The basic data structure of *Lisp* and of *Prolog* is the list.

Answers to questions

1 The diagonals AC and DB of the rectangle ABCD are of equal length because the triangles ADC and BCD, of which they are the hypotenuses, are congruent. The triangles are congruent because one pair of corresponding sides are the opposite sides of the rectangle, the second pair of corresponding sides are the other opposite sides of the rectangle, and the corresponding included angles are both right angles.

2 The angles ABC and ACB are equal because they are corresponding angles of the congruent triangles ABC and ACB. The triangles are congruent because AB = BC (given), BC = CB (common sense) and AC = AB (given).

3 length([], 0).
length([X | Tail], 1 + N) :- length(Tail, N).

4 delete(X, [X | Tail], Tail).
delete(X, [Head | Tail1], [Head | Tail2]):- delete(X, Tail1, Tail2).

5 (DEFINE   (APPEND L1 L2)
   (COND   (NULL(L1) L2)
            (T   (CONS (CAR L1) (APPEND (CDR L1) L2)))
   ))

6 (DEFINE   (MAP FN L)
   (COND   (NULL(L) ())
            (T   (CONS (FN (CAR L)) (MAP FN (CDR L))))
   ))

173

Annotated bibliography

Barr, A. and Feigenbaum, E. A. (Eds), *The Handbook of Artificial Intelligence, Volume 2*, Pitman, 1981.
Section 9 deals with applications of AI in education, and includes descriptions of tutorial systems.

Bratko, I., *Prolog Programming for Artificial Intelligence*, Addison-Wesley, 1986.
A careful introduction to *Prolog* as well as a full treatment of the language.

Friedman, D. P., *The Little Lisper*, Science Research Associates, 1974.
A mind-expanding introduction to recursion and, almost incidentally, to *Lisp*. The first edition is the most attractive.

Hart, A., *Knowledge Acquisition for Expert Systems*, Kogan Page, 1986.
Describes the methods commonly used for what this book has called knowledge elicitation.

Johnson, L. and Keravnou, E. T., *Expert Systems Technology: a Guide*, Abacus Press, 1985.
Provides detailed descriptions of the architecture and operation of a number of expert systems.

Townsend, C., *Mastering Expert Systems with TurboProlog*, Howard W. Sams, 1987.
How to write a simple expert system in *Prolog*.

Winston, P. H., *Artificial Intelligence* (2nd edition), Addison-Wesley, 1984.
Probably the best general introduction to AI.

Index

Action, 83
Advice-giving system, 7, 24–5, 45
Artificial intelligence, 1–4
Asking questions, 23, 44–5, 95, 135
Attribute, 65, 88

Backtracking, 18, 28–9, 161
Backward chaining, 97–8, 108, 144
Best-first search, 42–3, 54
Blocks world, 3, 14–16, 91
Breadth-first search, 41–2, 53
BUGGY, 138

C, 5
CASNET, 7, 113–17, 144
Certainty factor, 115–16, 144, 152
Chunk, 86, 104, 105
Clause, 99, 100, 158, 159–61
CLINAID, 122–4
Condition, 83, 160
Conditional function, 51, 52, 54
   in Lisp, 171
Confidence factor, *see* Certainty factor
Context tree, 108

Default, 88, 94, 95
Depth-first search, 40, 41, 53
Diagnosis, 7, 22–4, 107, 113, 118, 143, 149, 154
Dialogue, 135
   implied by system design, 23, 44, 45
   structure of, 44

Domain, 4, 61, 130

Example set, 61, 65, 71, 74
Expert system:
   applications, 2, 7–8
   architecture of, 30–1
   definition, 5
   evolution of, 4–5
   examples of, 107–26
   principles of operation, 11–29
   suitability, 6, 8
   as tutoring system, 130–6
Explanation of reasoning, 45, 131, 132

Facet, 94
Fact, 158
FORTRAN, 5, 158
Forward chaining, 97, 98
Frame, 94–6, 103–4, 119
Function, 48, 50–4, 170–1
   higher-level, 172
   type of, 49

Goal state, 15, 18, 20, 29
Graph, 35
   conversion to tree, 36–7
GUIDON, 137

Head, 50, 167
Heuristic, 8
How explanation, 131
Human-computer interface, 9, 30, 125

IDM, 120–2, 132
Inference, 58, 96–104, 108, 113, 121–2, 124, 148–50, 153–4
Inference engine, 30, 110, 115, 121
Inheritance, 87, 89, 99
Interface, 30, 125

Knowledge, 2, 57–80, 134–5, 162
  chunk, 86, 105
  sources of, 8
  structure of, 60, 104
  study of, 2, 9
Knowledge acquisition, 58
Knowledge base, 5, 30, 120, 121, 138–9
Knowledge-based system, 4
Knowledge elicitation, 58
  automatic, 64–74
  from an expert, 59–64
Knowledge engineer, 7
Knowledge representation, 58, 65–70, 82–3, 83–96, 145–7, 151–2

Laboratory data, 109, 112
Learning theory, 135, 136
Link, 95, 115
Lisp, 5, 169–72
List, 28, 50, 167, 169
List processing, 50–1, 167, 169, 170
Logic, 91–3, 100–3

Membership of a list, 51, 167
Microworld, 14
MYCIN, 7, 84, 107–13, 129, 137, 144

Near miss, 72, 74, 96, 104, 119, 130
Node, 12

Object, 87
  attribute-value triplet, 65, 88

PIP, 7, 118–20
Planning, 14–18

Problem solving, 4, 19–21
  for elicitation, 62
Prolog, 5, 158–68

Relation, 99, 145–7, 151–2
  operation on, 148–9, 153–4
Repertory grid, 63–4, 74–80
  analysis of, 78–80
Resolution, 100, 101–3
Rule, 12–13, 65–70, 83–6, 96–8, 109, 110, 131, 139, 144
  higher-level, 84–5
Rule-based system, 108, 113
R1, 6

Search, 15, 40, 41–4
  best-first, 42–3, 54
  breadth-first, 41–2, 53
  depth-first, 40, 41, 53
Semantic net, 87–90, 99–100, 113, 116
Shell, 5
Slot, 94–5, 104
State, 12
  representation, 19, 27
State space, 12
  form of, 35
  implicit description of, 39
  structure of, 33–4
State transition diagram, 12–13, 23, 26, 87, 114

Tableau, 92–3
Tail, 50, 167
TK!Solver, 124–6
Trace, 37, 43–4, 52, 54, 164, 166
Training examples, 61, 65, 71, 74
Tree, 35, 49
  for classification, 65–70
Tutoring system, 128–40
  architecture, 133–40
  history of, 129–30

Uncertainty, 7, 143–54

Why explanation, 131